Table of Contents

Table of Contents

Table of Contents

Foreword

The WorkForce Center (WFC) in south Minneapolis is one of the busiest in the state. In a neighborhood rich in ethnic restaurants and with a huge "global" indoor market just a short walk away, the WFC's diverse population visits every day to use computers and speak to job counselors in a large and open room, partly illuminated by the glow of monitors revealing job-seeking websites.

The south Minneapolis WFC serves thousands of job seekers annually. The first-floor crowd mainly works the Web. The story is different upstairs where, in a training room, at least 30 people patiently sat through a presentation on how to create a resume.

They range in age from their 20s and up. For some, the work of finding a job is a familiar situation, something they face every few years in a fast-changing job market.

For others, it was a new challenge, and they need to learn how to develop a resume and other assets that could eventually land them employment. One man, in the back of the room, turned out to be employed but took the class "just in case" he was laid off, representing a certain nervousness felt by many American workers in an unsettled era.

Welcome to the job market of the 21st century. "The average American today will work in five to eight fields and have an average of 18 jobs over a period of 40 to 60 years of their work life," says Paul Sears, a job counselor specialist in the south Minneapolis WFC. As companies shed jobs or change their production processes, others bulk up and hire. Having the right skills and attitude, says Sears, will help job seekers find new jobs, but they may have to change careers more than once — or twice, or three times.

In the training room, the participants share one singular desire: a job. And the resume class, one in an eight-part series, will help inform them of what employers want and expect as they describe their work lives on a one- or two-page document, along with a cover letter that they hope will draw the attention of managers assigned to hire new employees.

The other classes will give participants tips on finding hidden job markets, resumes, networking, researching companies, Internet job search strategies, interviews, thank you letters and other job-seeking skills. If you could not make the classes — and we highly suggest you sign up — you are lucky in one regard: You hold in your hands the book the WFC presenters use to guide participants through an extraordinary amount of information.

South Minneapolis operates just like Minnesota's other WorkForce Centers. Collectively, the employees of these centers are charged with the important duty of assisting Minnesotans in finding jobs. And one of the key assets they have used for more than two decades is "Creative Job Search" (CJS).

Since 1994, CJS has sold more than 11,000 copies not just in Minnesota but all over the United States, Europe, Australia and elsewhere. This edition covers several new and significant areas: career planning, finding a job when you are in the 50-plus age group and the emerging importance of social media in finding a job. We also included the stories of real job seekers and what strategies they used to land employment. Those job seekers say they found employment by using techniques they learned in WorkForce Center classes and from this book.

While CJS has plenty of Minnesota examples and resources, it also boasts information that will be relevant to readers in Richmond, Va., or even Rio de Janeiro. The core tools and skills in finding employment are borderless.

We hope you find this book helpful in your quest and, more to the point, we hope it leads to a good job for you in the future.

Finally, we would like to thank the subject experts and many other people who were involved in the writing, editing, and layout and design of this book. It was truly a collaborative effort.

We like to think that in this new edition we offer a menu of strategies, tactics and tools for a new age of job hunting.

CHAPTER 1

Career Planning

"Nobody can go back and start a new beginning, but anyone can start today and make a new ending."

— MARIA ROBINSON, WRITER

What are you going to do with the rest of your life? That's a good question to ponder at any age. It's probably on your mind if you are reading this book, attending a job search class or in a job that you don't like but cannot afford to leave — just yet. If you are unemployed you have some decisions to make, especially if you work in a career where the opportunities are diminishing and the road ahead looks bleak.

It's a good question, too, if you're a college graduate or a 30-something worker who isn't sure your career is headed in the right direction. It may be time for a change. Planning should even be embraced by job seekers who like their careers but may need to more sharply focus on where they want to go in their next jobs. After all, the career you have today could end in five years and you might have to shift to a new profession.

Robert Reich, former United States secretary of labor and current University of California at Berkeley economics professor, once had this to say about careers: "There are no longer career paths ... Careers paths are gone. They're not even trails. They're not even horse paths."

That's a bit of an exaggeration, of course, since career ladders still exist, though not nearly as many people spend enough time at any one firm — or in one profession — to climb them. And some careers are declining as they

Creative JOB SEARCH

are offshored to India, China, Mexico and other countries. Even information technology jobs have been impacted by the offshoring trend.

Career planning is the kind of issue that drives job seekers crazy. When do you know when to leave a career? It's like the old Clash song: "Should I Stay or Should I Go." Should you "recareer" or continue to look for opportunities in your field? Should you start your own business? The answers to those questions belong to you. We'll try to address some of those issues in this chapter to help you decide what comes next.

A Job No More

People who have lost their jobs potentially face significant emotional, psychological, financial and physical challenges. It is an unpleasant and difficult predicament, a trap door to anger and resentment, outrage and depression. To add to the injury, the jobless invariably face a bevy of insensitive assessments ("These things happen for a reason.") to time-worn clichés such as "I'm sure something better will come along."

Job loss can impact nearly every aspect of a person's life, from spending habits to self-esteem. Job loss can make people stronger, meeker, energized or demoralized. It can turn job seekers into small-business owners or consultants. It can spark ambition or extinguish it. And how anyone will handle a job loss cannot be always predicted. Most people will need some time to bounce back.

Managing Emotions and Psychological Stress

There's no doubt, regardless of whether you loved or hated your job, you will feel its loss. Lynn Joseph, the author of "The Job-Loss Recovery Guide" and manager of www.joblossrecovery.com, sees the following as constants following job loss: shock and denial, fear and anxiety, anger, bargaining, depression, acceptance and closure.

Joseph told the Washington Post she suggests a four-part process. First, "recognize your true feelings" and the anger inside you. Second, look for a safe outlet. Write your thoughts down. "Writing for 20 minutes a day over six days has been scientifically shown to lead to reframing difficult situations like job loss, new insights and even to landing a job sooner." Third, search for a sense of forgiveness, of yourself, or your former employer. You need not express it to your former boss, for example, but you must feel it in yourself. Fourth, change is going to come. The first three steps will lead to a better sense of yourself and prepare you for the work world again.

Financial Aspects of Unemployment

You will need to get your financial house in order. Minnesotans can find out how to apply for unemployment benefits by logging onto www.uimn.org. (Readers in other states should seek out their workforce agencies.) If applicable, try to get health coverage through your spouse's employer or parents. If that is not an option, sign up for COBRA (the Consolidated Omnibus Budget Reconciliation Act), which allows you to pay group rates for health insurance for a limited time. Be prepared for added expenses because you will be paying the full cost of the insurance without any funding from your former employer if your COBRA ends or if you do not have the option for COBRA coverage.

Should you receive a severance package, use it carefully. You have no idea how long you will remain unemployed. The key is to budget your money. What do you need to live? How much does your mortgage, rent, food, entertainment and transportation cost? What can you live without? The reality of your situation may force some hard choices about getting rid of certain expenses such as top tier cable television, eating out three times a week, going to movies or attending concerts and plays.

A strategy going forward is to cut extraneous costs early on just in case unemployment lasts longer than you assumed. The Web has excellent budgeting tools available for free or for relatively affordable subscriptions. Kiplinger's Magazine suggests the best are the following: Mint.com, Geezeo.com, Wesabe.com, BudgetTracker.com, BudgetPulse.com and Buxfer.com.

Physical Challenges

Unemployment can create health issues. Kate Strully, a scholar at the Harvard School of Public Health who conducted job loss research for the Robert Wood Johnson Foundation, says the odds of reporting poor to fair health increased 54 percent among people who lost jobs through no fault of their own. The odds of a new health condition increased by 83 percent among people who reported no pre-existing conditions prior to unemployment.

How can you avoid that? Build in an exercise regimen. Of all the expenses you may have, try to keep the health club membership. Or, use local recreation centers and the great outdoors to keep your body in shape. The tendency of job seekers is to surf the Web for any potential jobs, make networking calls, attend networking meetings and then find time to get in some exercise. Experts suggest setting that exercise time into your schedule early since it will help you deal with the stress and disillusionment of unemployment while preparing your mind and body for the rigors of job hunting.

A Career Planning Game Plan

Planning your next move demands self-examination and research before setting a job goal. Maybe you want to be a famous actor or a pop star? Go for it, but have a backup plan. If you're looking at a less risky career choice it may be time to look at what you've done and where you'd like to go and what you need to do to get there before starting the next chapter of your career.

There are bookshelves full of literature on career planning that generally agrees on a multi-step process to get people moving toward goals. Everyone has different experiences, desires and timelines. Yet a disorganized approach, for sure, will lead to frustration and disappointment rather than a focus on a new career. During this section we will reference other parts of this book since the principles of any job search remain largely the same, whether you're anxiously starting a different profession or staying in the same one.

Step One: Let's Talk About You

One simple step you can take in this direction is conducting a self-assessment. You can do this at one of Minnesota's WorkForce Centers through our employment counselors or through online assessment tests available at www.iseek.org, About.com (www.careerplanning. about.com) and other websites. The information gleaned from the test may put a damper on your plans to become an astronaut, but you may find some hidden skills and talents — leadership, communicating, working with tools, whatever — that will unlock ideas for new careers.

Job experts believe a good assessment includes interests, skills, values, preferred environments, temperament, motivations, work experience, training needs, and your current work and financial status. Each of these areas gives definition to your career search. Do you want a job with great regularity and little change, one with or without travel, with a large company, or a small one? Where creativity is rewarded? Or where doing diligently many of the same tasks daily is celebrated? Can you afford a new career? These are just some questions you will want to answer prior to thinking about heading in a new direction.

Avoid diminishing your creative impulse by placing too many limitations on it. "Don't let yourself get stuck in 'I can't do this, I can't do that' kinds of thinking that reflect only current real-world constraints but not what could be developed," argues Leonard Lang, a Minneapolis-based career coach and author of "Guide to Lifework: Working with Integrity and Heart." "By thinking creatively, you can be re-energized and find new solutions you hadn't dreamed of before. But that won't happen if you get stuck on thinking first of these constraints, such as there are bills to pay ... kids are in school ... 'I don't have the education.' Dealing with those constraints is vital after you get a vision of your career."

Time for Homework

Armed with a greater sense of yourself through personal and professional assessments, you now have to begin a major research project. Later in this book, we offer you a myriad of places on the Web and at the library where you can explore careers that you find appealing and that may fit your skill set — or your skill set with additional training.

Follow a strategy of studying the demand for occupations you find attractive. You will be advised to "follow your bliss" in career books and on the Web. That's an option — maybe you could find a career transforming your skills as an amateur taxidermist into a professional one. Just don't make the decision blindly. Understand that a new career may entail sometimes considerable financial sacrifice.

By doing your homework, you might want to consider a career in the top 20 or 30 growing professions rather than strike out on an unlikely dream of becoming, well, a brain surgeon at age 55. No career counselor wants to dampen enthusiasm, but a dose of reality is often required unless a person really possesses the absolute drive and determination to take on an exceptionally challenging profession.

One job expert related the story of a woman who really did want to become a physician at age 40 and understood the sacrifices and time it would take to embark upon a medical career. She went with her passion. That's an extraordinary story, and a rare one. More commonplace are people who develop skills in one area that they can repurpose in another field.

Rather than rehash a later chapter of this book, we will refer you to Chapter 2 for details on occupations, conducting labor market surveys, reaching out for informational interviews and finding job survey data.

Filling Skill Gaps

Once you have a pretty good idea of what career or careers you want to pursue, you may find your lack of knowledge or skills will make it hard for you to find employment. Let's say you sold medical products to hospitals for a number of years and want to transition into a role where you're a care provider, such as Licensed Practical Nurse or Registered Nurse. You will need additional schooling in order to make that dramatic a leap.

Perhaps you seek a different career path in the same or a similar profession. A programmer who wants to get into management could consider a master's of business degree or a leadership/executive training program at a local college. That programmer could volunteer for managerial-style jobs with an IT association to experience, in a small way, the skills demanded of a larger managerial position in the future.

You can, in effect, conduct your own "skill gap analysis" to determine what education, degrees and training — or combination of all three — might be needed in a different career. Then you need to find the education or training you require for your new career, an issue less of a problem in large or medium-sized cities where many colleges and private institutions have created night and weekend courses and degrees for working adults. (If you're unemployed you may qualify for financial assistance and be able to attend day classes.)

Making a Move

You may decide, in the end, to stay in your current profession or to take whatever positions come your way, a strategy not without appeal in a job-poor economy. You could come to the conclusion that you'd prefer your favorite activities remain hobbies instead of potentially new careers or that you devote your ancillary talents to volunteer organizations instead of professional, paying positions.

More than a few brilliant amateur photographers have not opened studios, for instance, and many great teachers remain mentors and tutors at schools and have not gone into the profession. Your talents beyond work always can be exercised in other avenues.

In many cases staying in your field will be a wise choice. Not everyone can, or should, start a new career. The question you have to answer in moving in a different direction is whether you can continue in your profession. Can you still find a job or contract work? And if you're starting anew, do you have the commitment and resilience required to make what will be a monumental change fraught with the potential for considerable setbacks, roadblocks, challenges and struggles?

Lang suggests people test drive their vision. Take a course or two in the career you want to pursue, rather than entering a full-time degree program. A few courses later you might decide that teaching elementary school isn't something you want to do, after all. Or, you find your commitment has solidified and to save time you're going to become a full-time student. Investing time in courses or training will give you a clearer picture of whether a new career is what you really want.

If you have to take a temporary job while retraining or preparing for a new profession, "this is nothing to feel bad about," adds Lang, who has spoken at Minnesota WorkForce Centers. "It may be that a transitional job will give you experience or connections that help you move toward your larger goal."

Road-weary from spending as many as four months a year on the road and looking for a chance to spend more time with her two children, Mary Beth Heffernan decided to take a break from corporate America.

After having spent 18 years building a global footprint for a Twin Cities biomedical company, she went home to two young children and to volunteer. She signed on to help Second Harvest, a local food shelf, starting as an envelope stuffer and then moving up to managing groups that came to pack groceries for food shelves.

For more than a year Heffernan enjoyed contributing to an organization committed to helping others in their time of need. After hinting that she might be interested in actually working for Second Harvest, an executive interviewed her for the job of donor relations manager.

She joined Second Harvest in 2008, this time as an employee. "The pieces fell together for me during the 14 months I was off," says Heffernan. "I told the people who interviewed me I was looking to work in a nonprofit. It's less frantic than working for a public company, where you have to meet your goals quarterly, but there are more deadlines because there is more to do with fewer people."

If you take the plunge into a new career, you will not be alone. A January 2010 Minneapolis Star Tribune feature story revealed many career changers, among them an airline mechanic studying to become a biomedical technician, a project manager who opened a consignment store, a used car dealer who sells his own homemade salsa at area grocery stores and farmers markets, a former assistant principal taking classes to become a computer technician and a recruiter at Target who left that job to pursue a singing career.

The Path of Independence

For many job seekers a return to the 9 to 5 existence, even in a new profession, fails to excite the imagination or to create a firm desire to move in that direction. Many people may like their professions but simply no longer want a boss, or to work for others. The jobs in their field may have dried up even if the work has not. They may be ready to become "consultants" or "independent contractors" or work solo or with small groups of other individuals on projects.

Thousands of people earn a living in Minnesota as independent contractors. Some of them team up to create small agencies and businesses; others prefer to remain on their own. Several professions lend themselves to an independent approach, among them marketing, public relations, advertising, journalism (or freelance/contract writing), information technology, architecture, technical writing, home building and repair, plumbing, law and research. In whatever profession you're in, there's a good chance your company has used or is employing contractors who have their own business.

Independent contractors face many challenges. They have to market their own products and services, network constantly, cold call if necessary, and meet and exceed client expectations on a routine basis because of — usually — stiff competition from other contractors. Turn in bad work and you will get no more work. If an employee is struggling, managers generally provide them counseling, training and a second chance. They have no obligation to provide that to independent contractors and generally will not unless the parties have had a long established relationship. Great devotion to clients is often necessary.

There are other issues. Contractors and small-business owners have to pay for their own medical insurance, a huge cost center. Other benefits common in full-time employment — disability insurance, pre-tax deductions, 401(k)s and other retirement vehicles — must be self-funded. You're on your own. Services such as accounting and contracting must be done in-house or handled by another firm. The responsibilities are much greater than working for someone else.

So what are the advantages? Ask any small-business owner or contractor and they will probably speak to the issue of freedom, the upside in some professions of a significantly higher income than a paid position, fewer limitations on vacation or sick time, greater flexibility in raising a family (or indulging in other non-work interests) and a much wider variety of work. There is an indescribable sensation of achievement in earning every dollar of your income through your own effort, from finding clients to completing a project to maintaining good client relationships.

It has been called the American dream. And for millions of Americans, it is a dream come true. No longer are contractors "between opportunities" and dismissed as tiny players in a big economy. They are the largest job generation machine in the United States and will continue to be in the 21st century. Still, running any kind of business demands a high level of ambition, risk tolerance, attention to detail and professional skill.

This dream is not for everyone, nor should it be. Starting a small business, however, may become one of the few options left for job seekers, especially those in the later stages of their careers. And it remains a way for people to create their own careers and achieve a finer work-life balance instead of having their fate determined by the whims of employers.

Living With the Decision

You will have to live with your decision for some time, so make it wisely. Once you have committed to a new direction, stay the course for a while because success will not happen overnight, or even after a year. It's likely to take a while to earn a degree, absorb training or sell your product or services. Then, it will take time to find the employment you seek.

If an opportunity arises in your former profession, it may leave you at a crossroads. Whether to take the offer presents a dilemma, especially if you miss your former work. Should you recall that work with a significant anxiousness and dread, you will want to take great consideration prior to making a decision. Can you live with going back, especially if you need the money? Or is it better to soldier on?

Most career changers will never have that option since they cease sending out resumes and looking in their fields. Others may entertain a few phone calls with offers. And then they'll have to decide whether to continue the new plan or retrench and head back to the comfort of a job and a career they once knew.

CHAPTER 2

Preparing for the Job Hunt

"Woke up, fell out of bed, dragged a comb across my head, found my way downstairs and drank a cup ..."

—"A DAY IN THE LIFE," JOHN LENNON AND PAUL McCARTNEY

The Beatles may have been singing of the life of an average day of a typical British worker circa late 1960s, but if you're a job seeker take heed: You, too, need to get out of bed, have a cup and hit the computer and the phone to continue your search. A successful job search requires organization, effort and self-discipline.

If you are used to having someone else organize your activities, you will be mastering new skills that will require you to stay focused, avoid distractions and stay the course, despite potentially rough waters on the voyage to employment. Start with a few good habits and practices right away to avoid getting caught in a cycle where you fritter away time without any attempt to keep yourself focused and accountable to the goal of finding a job.

Getting Organized

A successful job search requires effort. That means getting organized, scheduling time for tasks and keeping a record of your achievements or mileposts ("made seven cold calls today," "had an informational interview").

Managing a Schedule

Successful job seekers have mastered the art of managing their schedules and establishing measurable goals. For example, commit a block of hours every day for searching and identifying companies you want to contact and jobs you want to apply for. Consider a schedule in which every Monday morning you conduct Internet searches that at minimum result in the names of 10 new employers. Tuesday's goal could be contacting the 10 employers you identified Monday. Tuesday morning might be a good time to reach employers, from 9 to 11 a.m., for example.

You should set some goals for your search. The toughest thing about being unemployed is the lack of accountability to anyone but yourself. That's why joining a networking group or reporting progress to a friend, spouse or partner makes certain sense. It's relatively easy to get sidetracked during a job search by spending valuable hours surfing the Internet. Strange curiosities and searches that take you into informational netherworlds can consume endless hours. Filling an eight-hour work day without a job can be remarkably easy. Remember the sports proverb: Keep your eye on the ball.

Of course, all work and no play will make for irritability. If you have reached out to 20 employers during a week and had a few networking events and interviews, offer yourself a reward involving your passions or interests. A movie. A walk in the park. An afternoon at a museum. And then start the search anew.

Keeping Records

During the job-search process you may make hundreds of contacts and generate new opportunities for part-time and full-time work. You need to maintain a filing system to organize your progress. A variety of systems are available including computer filing systems, alphabetized three-ring binders or notebooks. Choose the system that makes the most sense to you.

A "contact tracker," as some job experts call it, will assist in creating a database of people and companies you have called, e-mailed and sent your resume and cover letter during a search. Keep records of when you make contacts, who you called, their e-mails, addresses and websites. Just because a company turned you down doesn't mean it won't become a prospect in the future. A general rule in sales is that it takes at least three contacts to turn a prospect into a client. That may not be true when seeking a position with a company: Hitting them half a dozen times with phone calls and letters may not work at all. Or, you may be working for that company someday soon.

In the bestselling "Knock 'em Dead: The Ultimate Job Search Guide, 2010," author Martin Yate writes: "As you get your job search up to speed, the number of baited hooks you have in the water will grow dramatically. The resumes you send out will require follow-up calls, and the networking and research calls you make to potential employees will create the need to mail out resumes, which in return will generate more follow-up calls. Without tracking mechanisms in place this can quickly get out of hand. It would be crazy to make this effort to get your job search and career management plan functioning and then let important opportunities fall through the cracks for lack of attention to detail."

Researching Employers

N ow that you have an idea for organizing your job search you can begin conducting research in order to find openings and employers you seek to work for in the future. By researching an industry, occupation or employer, you gain a better understanding of job availability, company culture, potential growth of businesses and industries, and how your skills could be applied to a different profession, if that becomes a necessity.

Finding out about potential employers gives you a chance to measure your qualifications against those required by a particular company. They force you to determine whether you need more training in a certain area and whether the skills you have match the talent employers want.

Structuring Research

When beginning your research, start gathering information on specific occupations, industries, individual companies and job availability in your area. Your research will naturally become more specific as you gain momentum. Company websites, career information resources, trade journals and online job boards are all good resources for discovering what experience, training and knowledge are required by employers.

Create an online or paper filing system containing research pertaining to companies you want to reach. That way, you don't have to rely on Google every time you want to look over the content you found last week on the target of your research. Sometimes articles mysteriously disappear or land much further down the list of hits on search engines; better to print it out, send a copy to your e-mail account or cut and paste content into a Word document.

What should you look for? Study a company's products or services, size, history, location(s) (especially in relationship to where you live), mission statement or philosophy (or "value proposition" if such a document exists) and financial situation, as well as potential for growth. You should dig a little deeper and find out what changes the employer has undergone in the last five years and what kind of human resource policies it has, from flex time to a commitment to provide community services.

Finally, always read the "press" section on websites, sometimes called "news and events." This is where the company will be revealing potentially great information to job seekers, such as plant expansions, new product roll-outs, or sponsorship of events. An expanding workforce may show up in a press release but not in local wanted ads.

RESOURCES FOR RESEARCH

Listed below are some of the many resources that have information about employers.

- Minnesota WorkForce Center Resource Area staff or staff at your local state employment service

- People working with the employer

- Current newspapers, trade journals and business magazines and newspapers. (In the Twin Cities, Finance and Commerce and The Business Journal are good examples of publications with stories about growing employers.)

- Employer websites

- Articles in Internet publications containing information that relates to industries, occupations or employers

- Social networking services, blogs and company employee sites (Some independent employee sites are interesting because they offer insights not found on "official" employer sites.)

- Libraries, which have special sections on occupations, careers and job search information, article databases, business publications, business directories and other resources

- College placement offices and alumni associations

- Chamber of Commerce or Jaycees

- Annual reports

- Employer newsletters and brochures available from the employer's public relations office or personnel department

The same information will make you look good should you get an interview in which you can show how well-informed you are by saying, "I noticed you're opening a new plant in Kentucky …" or "I'm really intrigued by that new product you released, the biodegradable coffee cup …" Companies not only appreciate that you found them through diligent research, they are equally impressed when you display knowledge of their recent actions and address issues within their industries.

Labor Market Survey

Labor market surveys are tools that can help determine if an occupation or specific line of work is appropriate for you. Labor market surveys can be effective because they can help you gain insights into fields and occupations.

The pace of business is so fast today that calling people and asking questions about their occupations may result in few call-backs or answered e-mails. The Internet has voluminous amounts of information on careers, potential job openings in those occupations and even reflections or articles by bloggers, journalists and others that describe what it is like to work in a field. Many job search books have suggestions on doing a labor market survey even though it seems unlikely, given the pressures of an average workday, that many people have the time to answer a series of questions from someone they have never met.

If you want to conduct a labor market survey, try to keep it in your network of contacts so you at least have an opening when making that call: "Jim Schmidt told me to give you a call. I'm interested in working at 3M and want to learn more about the company's culture," sounds better than "I want to work at 3M. Can you tell me what it's like to work there?"

Be clear, be precise, tell the individual you will not take up more than a few minutes of his or her time and hope for a return call. Keep in mind not everyone will tell the truth about an employer to a total stranger, even one recommended by a friend. You may gain some insights or you might find the practice of labor market surveys a waste of time in an age when so much information about companies is widely available on the Internet and at your local library.

A Deeper Data Dive

If you know the specific occupation or line of work that interests you, consult the Occupational Information Network (O*Net), Minnesota Career Information System (MCIS) or the Bureau of Labor Statistics websites (www.bls.gov). Other reference books are available at Minnesota WorkForce Centers or your local state employment office, public libraries, technical schools, colleges and universities.

Libraries are a great place to access databases that may not be available for free on the Internet. In Minnesota anyone with a library card can register with the Hennepin County Public Library system and then access its vast repository of online databases. Other library systems may have similar arrangements. The following are among the best business databases:

- **Business & Company Resource Center:** Searchable by industry or name, it offers nearly everything you'd want to know about thousands of companies.

- **Business Source Premier:** The database holds economic data, company profiles, industry information, market research reports and much more.

- **ReferenceUSA:** The directory of U.S.-based businesses provides a way to search by business name, industry, city, county and ZIP code while offering a panoply of information.

These databases are available online, too, but the fees charged for their use is often substantial. That's why it's better to physically go to the library to use them or to register so you can gain Web access with a library card.

LABOR MARKET SURVEY SOURCES

- Minnesota Department of Employment and Economic Development, Research and Statistics Labor Market Information Help Line at 651.259.7384, or e-mail (deed.lmi@state.mn.us)

- ISEEK (www.iseek.org), a Minnesota-based job information site with posted openings

- Minnesota Career Information System (mncis.intocareers.org)

- Bureau of Labor Statistics (www.bls.gov)

- Occupational Information Network (O*Net) (online.onetcenter.org)

- Hoover's Online (www.hoovers.com) or Vault (www.vault.com) are go-to sites for larger publicly (and privately) traded companies

You can also tap into social networking sites for content on jobs. In that setting there may be members of networking groups willing to offer you insights into a particular field. Networking groups in an occupation such as project management or medical technology or communications are great settings in which to glean insider knowledge and observations of what is required of practitioners in that industry, training, openings, salaries and so forth.

Smaller Market Research

If you live in a small or medium-sized city, the kind of extensive research described in this chapter may not be all that relevant. You probably know a lot about the major employers, and the smaller ones are not going to be part of any of the national databases found on the Web or in libraries. Where does that leave you?

The best basic research you can do is to get the names of small employers, study their websites and see if they list jobs. Should the management team be listed, take a look and see if you recognize any names. In a small town they may be members of your church or have children at your school. Even if you don't know them, try to call or e-mail them. Chances are they probably have a little more time to chat with a job seeker than their larger corporate counterparts.

You can also employ something as simple as the Yellow Pages. Look at the companies in your profession, or a profession you seek to join, and take down their names, addresses and phone numbers. If your community's Yellow Pages provider has an online directory, use that because companies listed sometimes have a link directly to their website — if they have one.

Another research source is the website of your local newspaper and the closest regional daily newspaper. At those sites you can usually do searches of companies and see what kinds of stories have been written about them. Even smaller firms, if they are growing or offer intriguing products and services, may have had articles written about them.

Since many small dailies and weeklies don't have extensive archives on the Web, you will have to go to your local library to search for copies or, alternatively, call the newspaper itself. Many of them file stories by subject matter and are willing to share those with local residents as long as they don't take them from the premises.

 Minnesota has two fine resources for job seekers, noted earlier, in MinnesotaWorks.net and www.iseek.org. You can look for positions through a ZIP code search and let the search engine know how many miles you are willing to commute. Depending on where you live you may have to extend the search out to find the kind of job you desire.

Finally, the best research for job seekers in smaller communities comes in networking with friends, family, neighbors and other acquaintances. Great research, especially on smaller employers, just isn't available. That's where cold-calling — dealt with in Chapter 6 — and networking will be exceptionally important to your research. In the yin and yang of job hunting, smaller markets have the same advantage and disadvantage: a limited number of employers that you will have to research and contact, yet a smaller number of available jobs.

ENDNOTES

JOB SEARCH SCHEDULE SAMPLE							
Week of September 7							
Time	**Sunday**	**Monday**	**Tuesday**	**Wednesday**	**Thursday**	**Friday**	**Saturday**
8:00 a.m.	Shower and dress. Read the newspaper.	Shower and dress by 8:30. Set goals for the day/week.	Same as Monday.	Same as Monday.	Same as Monday.	Same as Monday.	Go to the farmers market.
9:00 a.m.	Read Sunday paper. Check online for newspaper job ads by 9:30.	Respond by phone to Sunday ads.	Make networking calls.	Return calls. Schedule appointments.	Attend job club.	Return calls. Schedule appointments.	
10:00 a.m.	Take a walk, play with the kids, etc.	Get information for writing responses to ads. Go to the Minnesota WorkForce Center.	Make networking calls.	Attend job fair.	Attend job club	Make networking calls.	
11:00 a.m.	Have some fun!	Write cover letters. Make changes on resume.	Return phone calls. Schedule appointments.		Do informational interview.		
12:00 p.m.	Lunch	Lunch	Lunch	Lunch	Lunch	Lunch	Lunch
1:00 p.m.		Appointment	Appointment	Check out Minnesota WorkForce Center computer.	Appointment	Research the employer for the interview next week.	
2:00 p.m.		Appointment	Appointment	Call on leads obtained at Minnesota WorkForce Center.	Appointment	Research the employer for the interview next week.	
3:00 p.m.		Appointment	Appointment	Appointment		Research the employer for the interview next week.	
4:00 p.m.		Walk	Walk	Walk	Walk	Walk	
5:00 p.m.		Evaluate today. Review tomorrow. Send thank you notes.	Same as Monday.	Same as Monday.	Same as Monday.	Same as Monday and review the week.	

JOB SEARCH SCHEDULE							
Week of _____							
Time	Sunday	Monday	Tuesday	Wednesday	Thursday	Friday	Saturday
8:00 a.m.							
9:00 a.m.							
10:00 a.m.							
11:00 a.m.							
12:00 p.m.							
1:00 p.m.							
2:00 p.m.							
3:00 p.m.							
4:00 p.m.							
5:00 p.m.							

JOB LEAD

No matter where you get your job leads, it is important to keep track of them. Follow up on each lead. They may provide you with other job leads. Ask for other contacts or leads.

Employer:	
Contact Person:	
Address:	
Phone:	
E-mail/Fax Address:	
Position:	
Source of Job Lead:	
Response:	
Date Sent or Faxed Resume :	
Follow-up Date:	
Results and Other Useful Information:	

NOTES

CHAPTER 3

Identifying Your Skills

"*Although people are accused of not knowing their own weakness, yet perhaps few know their own strength. It is in people as in soils, where sometimes there is a vein of gold which the owner knows not of.*"

— JONATHAN SWIFT

Highlighting your skills in resumes, cover letters and interviews is part of the foundation of a successful job search.

Employers want to know more than your past job titles. They want to know your talents and what you have done with them. If you were to purchase a product that would cost thousands of dollars annually, you would want to know how its features could help you.

Many people have a hard time identifying their skills. Don't think of a skill as something that requires years of formal education and experience to develop. A skill is something you are doing right now in your life. In fact, job experts such as Richard Bolles suggest the average person has between 500 and 800 identifiable skills, an impressive figure, though no employer will want to hear every one of them. Instead, you need to identify at least 10 to 20 employer-attracting skills worthy of mention and bolstered by evidence of accomplishment on your resume.

There's a method to identifying, describing and promoting your skill set that we'll now investigate.

What are You Good At?

One way to think about skills is to consider yourself a product and employers as consumers. What skills are going to be of use in a particular job or company? What product attributes do you bring to the table? What problem can you solve for an employer?

Think hard about your career, life and interests and then examine the lists we've created in the following pages to guide you in your skill-identifying journey.

Take a good look at yourself. Consider your personality. Good at self-management? Are you punctual, dependable, creative, independent, flexible and ambitious? Good for you. You just listed six skills.

Work in an office on a computer? That's not just one skill, it's many: typing, writing, editing and meeting deadlines. A computer programmer troubleshooting a network failure uses proofreading skills to find errors in computer codes. A cook uses slicing and cleaning skills to prepare vegetables. To complete tasks in the course of our daily lives, we balance checking accounts, manage budgets, shop and drive.

Those are skills.

Some of those skills are employed at jobs, others in life. Some can be used in resumes and during interviews. Others will be irrelevant. Blowing square bubbles and telling jokes are great party antics, but not so great for serious job interviews unless, of course, you're applying to a comedy troupe or the circus. Understanding skills improves your ability to identify them.

Job Skills

Job skills are specific to a job or occupation. An administrative assistant is skilled in typing, word processing, filing, answering telephones and drafting correspondence. An accountant's skills include calculating accounts receivable and accounts payable, preparing taxes and using computer accounting programs. A marketer's skills revolve around working with creative teams, developing plans for product rollouts, presenting work in front of clients, working with various vendors and meeting deadlines.

Behind most skills lies a body of knowledge. A graphic designer knows how to create documents using Adobe's InDesign from files created in Microsoft Word. A cook knows about cooking techniques such as basting or baking. An auto mechanic is trained to fix problems in cars from eight or 10 manufacturers or more.

TRANSFORMING EVERYDAY ACTIVITIES INTO SKILLS

Here are a few examples of home-based activities and other occupations that can fit a skill resume.

Shopping: Planning/ organizational skills, budgeting, time management, product evaluation and nutrition.

Yard Work/Lawn Care: Physical endurance/coordination, equipment maintenance, safety operations, chemical applications, goal setting.

Administrative Assistant: Typing, word processing, tactfulness, timeliness, responsible, creative, dependable, detail-oriented, sincere, meeting deadlines, communicating, helping others, problem solving, checking for accuracy, researching, writing clearly and concisely.

Answering Telephones: Listening, mediating, communicating, respectful, helpful, resolving conflict, developing rapport, assertiveness, dependable, outgoing, pleasant, sensitive, tolerant, detail-oriented, enthusiastic, friendly, intelligent, kind, mature, patient, sincere, tactful, understanding.

Job skills do not always come from employment. They may be developed through education, hobbies, community activities and life experiences. Common activities such as shopping, managing finances, leading a committee at a school, volunteering or teaching are activities that involve potential job skills.

Job skills are important to employers because they are often looking for individuals with specific talents. They may want someone who is a team player, learns fast, handles little structure, loves challenges, enjoys pursuing goals and has an agreeable personality. They may also want that same individual to have specific skills, such as working with particular software programs or the ability to drive a certain class of vehicle or operate a piece of machinery. Mix those skills together for the right employer and you will find yourself employed.

CASE STUDY
RESTAURANT MANAGER

A culinary manager for 20 years, Stan was laid off and looking for a job. Working with an employment counselor specialist in Marshall, Minn., Stan identified a host of transferable skills: time management, budgeting, employee relations, negotiating and scheduling. He managed banquets as large as 500 people and understood supply chain management and logistics.

Restaurants, of course, are customer-service oriented — at least the successful ones — and require employees to have good communication skills and a touch of human relations management. Stan had covered all that ground, and much more, in his time in the industry.

Stan put together a resume strong on transferable skills, and they put it on a well-known job board, where someone at an automotive service center chain saw it. The chain's vice president called Stan to ask him to come in for an interview and heard this response: "My only experience with grease and oil is cooking it."

In the end, Stan wasn't interested in the job. He wound up back in the food and service industry and eventually landed a managerial position he loves. The initial skepticism about transferable skills has evaporated, and he now looks for them in applicants who might not have much in the way of a food service background but do have the necessary abilities to potentially succeed, as he did, in the field.

Transferable Skills

Many talents can be applied to a variety of activities. They can transfer from one activity to another. Self-management ability and job-specific skills are transferable. If you can operate a drill press, you have skills to operate other types of machinery. If you can balance a personal bank account, you have the math aptitude to balance a business account. If you coordinate events, lead meetings, participate on teams or get involved in community activities, you have several leadership competencies that could transfer to a job.

In essence, transferable skills are proficiencies developed in a profession, previous employment or volunteer or hobby activities. For job seekers who want to try a different career, transferable skills will be a big deal on their resumes because their work histories alone might not convince employers they can flourish in a new environment. The transferable skills they delineate on their resumes will have to offer a compelling argument for their consideration.

That makes transferable skills all the more important for many reasons. Many job seekers are unlikely to find a job identical to their previous employment. Therefore, carefully evaluating how your skills transfer into other opportunities is critical. People seeking their first job, making a major career change or returning to employment after a long absence will mostly use transferable skills in their job search.

Self-Management Skills

These are skills you use day-to-day to get along with others. They are the skills that make you unique. Examples of self-management skills are sincerity, reliability, tactfulness, patience, flexibility, timeliness and tolerance. Alongside those skills are motivation, persistence, drive and cooperation.

Do not underestimate self-management skills, especially if they show motivation and a good work attitude. These abilities are especially important for people who are seeking their first job or returning to employment after an absence.

Emotional Intelligence

Are you able to manage your own emotions and instinctively understand or detect those of colleagues, friends and acquaintances? You may be blessed with emotional intelligence, another discipline in the evolving skills toolset that has gained traction ever since Daniel Goleman put the term on the map in his bestselling 1995 book "Emotional Intelligence: Why It Can Matter More Than IQ."

Defining it isn't all that easy. Peter Salovey and John Mayer, two leading experts on emotional intelligence who have authored several books on the topic, put it this way: "We define emotional intelligence as the subset of social intelligence that involves the ability to monitor one's own and others' feelings and emotions, to discriminate among them and to use this information to guide one's thinking and actions."

Emotional intelligence isn't just essential in the workplace. It's also an important trait to possess during the job hunt, especially when setbacks occur. Being able to find the energy to send out one more resume, make one more call, hit that networking meeting another time speaks not only to persistence but to the ability to manage your own emotions and not be defeated by them. Job hunting can be incredibly difficult, and staying positive and engaged in the process can be daunting. Yet it is the key to your success. And it requires emotional intelligence.

Closer Look

GETTING A GRIP ON EMOTIONAL INTELLIGENCE

On a more global scale, one Twin Cities company that has embraced emotional intelligence is Ameriprise Financial, led by its executive vice president, Doug Lennick, co-author of "Moral Intelligence: Enhancing Business Performance and Leadership Success." Ameriprise, of course, employs thousands of financial planners who have to deal with a roller coaster of emotions, from dealing with people who may speak to them several times before turning down their services to delivering bad news to clients about slow markets and declining stock prices.

Lennick and emotional intelligence advocates believe you can train your brain to deal with the stress of disappointment and to nurture resilience. Those qualities are especially valuable in sales positions, but they have to be maintained during your job hunt, too, since much of what you will be doing involves selling yourself, a challenge that may cause episodes of disillusionment even in the most resilient among us. Emotional intelligence means if a letter comes with a "sorry you didn't get the position" line, you keep networking and looking for a job.

Skills Versus Job Training

St. Paul Pioneer Press columnist and career consultant Amy Lindgren has an interesting take on job training. In a column published in November 2009, she says that job training only "approximates" what employers need and that most jobs require talents well beyond what any class or certificate program offers.

"Employers hire workers to DO something, not to BE something," she writes. "That is, they need you to perform tasks, not to simply be certified whatever. Obvious, but easy to forget."

Her approach? If you need a license to do a job, get one. If being certified might help you find a job, take short-term classes and look for contract assignments or other hands-on experiences. Look for volunteer opportunities. Or take on a few do-it-yourself gigs to reveal your talents in a field.

And do not undertake a skills-building effort in the dark. Talk to employers, says Lindgren. "By identifying the organizations you'd like to work for and then speaking with managers about the skills they need, you'll be able to focus on the true goal, which is to be skilled and employable, not simply trained."

Developing Skills While Looking for a Job

You should consider spending time developing new skills through volunteering. Don't volunteer, of course, only for that reason. Yet be mindful that community organizations need help, and you have plenty to offer while you try out new career options, experiences and, potentially, leadership roles.

FOUR STEPS TOWARD IDENTIFYING YOUR SKILLS

Step 1: Write the title of an employment-related activity. Focus on those activities that potentially demonstrate skill and experience relative to employment. You may get these titles from skills you gained while working for community organizations, volunteer activities and employers.

Step 2: List the tasks involved in performing this activity. Tasks are the basic functions of an activity.

Step 3: List the skills involved in accomplishing each task. Be sure to include job, self-management and transferable skills.

Step 4: Network with friends, associates and family. Ask them what skills they see that you have.

Every community usually has an organization — United Way is a major one — that helps people find volunteer opportunities. In larger cities, the openings are fairly numerous in most cases. Check your community newspaper, too, because many have a weekly feature listing volunteer opportunities in your neighborhood or your city.

In the Twin Cities, the following organizations are set up to match volunteers: Volunteer Match (www.volunteermatch.org), Greater Twin Cities United Way (www.unitedwaytwincities.org) and Hands on Twin Cities (www. handsontwincities.org).

Self-Branding

"We are the CEOs of our own companies: Me Inc."

— TOM PETERS, MANAGEMENT CONSULTANT

Using the list of skills you have identified in this chapter, you can put them to work by developing what is called a "self-brand." You are not just a job seeker or a face in the crowd. Tom Peters first suggested the concept in a 1997 article in Fast Company magazine, and ever since then a cottage industry of consultants has popped up to help job seekers self-brand, along with a host of books and magazine articles devoted to the topic.

Your skills make up a multi-faceted business that provides an essential service to your clients (employers). When a new brand is launched, the company thinks about what makes its product unique. Next, it creates a campaign to convince people that your brand is the best to fill a position.

Savvy job seekers will think of themselves in a similar way. What makes me unique? How can I convince employers I am the best candidate for this job? Self-branding is valuable to a job search because it helps you define who you are. Simply, it is the process by which individuals identify and communicate their unique skills to others.

Developing a Self-Brand

Dan Schawbel, author of "Me 2.0: Build a Powerful Brand to Achieve Career Success," suggests a four-step process for self-branding: discover, create, communicate, maintain.

Discover starts with determining what you want in a job or career.

Create and *communicate* focus on resumes, online profiles, blogs, Twitter and Facebook, all potential portfolio material for your "brand tool kit."

Maintain deals with monitoring how your brand is noted, an easy thing to do with Google Alert (www.google.com/alert) and other Web-based tracking sites. You'll want to know what others are saying about you, and if it's wrong you can correct those impressions quickly.

A few other points about self-branding: You have to be consistent. You have to contribute to various online media to keep your name and brand fresh, whether it is through a personal blog or a Facebook contribution.

You have to get out of the house. While a lot of self-branding occurs online, the majority happens in real time. You have to attend networking functions, conferences and informational interviews. Press the flesh and hand out plenty of business cards with your website, blog and phone number. If you wish, list the social networking sites you use so that contacts can "friend" you or become your follower on Twitter.

In addition, if you develop a self-brand you must also accept the responsibility to keep it up. While self-branding is helpful during your job search, it needs to continue evolving even after you have won a new job. Make sure your "tools" are always honest and updated. Your self-brand will evolve as you gain new skills. But take care not to spend company time nurturing your personal brand on the job, which can be grounds for your boss showing you the door.

A Final Note on Self-Branding

As self-branding has risen to prominence it seems many of its practitioners are Web-savvy self-promoters largely in the media, marketing, public relations and technology. A word to the wise: Are others in your field self-branding? If you're looking for a job, do employers appreciate your ability to blog, to maintain a cool website, to stay abreast of social media?

If not, and if you're not going into self-employed consulting, it may be better to focus your efforts on other activities.

ENDNOTES: Listing Attributes

*T*he next section focuses on lists of skills you can use to describe your talents. These can be deployed on a resume, in cover letters and in conversations with various employers. Obviously, your career and personality won't fit all these attributes, and if they do you're being dishonest.

GENERAL TRAITS

What kind of person are you? General traits describe you, not just as a worker bee, but as a human being. The descriptive words offered below will give you an idea of the many positive things you can say about yourself.

Able	Dutiful	Kind	Pleasant
Accepting	Efficient	Knowledgeable	Poised
Active	Ethical	Liberal	Powerful
Adaptable	Extroverted	Lively	Precise
Ambitious	Fair	Logical	Principled
Assertive	Frank	Loving	Progressive
Bold	Friendly	Maternal	Protective
Bright	Thrifty	Mature	Questioning
Calm	Gentle	Modest	Quiet
Caring	Giving	Mystical	Rational
Certain	Helpful	Observant	Realistic
Cheerful	Honorable	Organized	Reasonable
Clever	Idealistic	Original	Reassuring
Confident	Imaginative	Passive	Reflective
Courageous	Independent	Paternal	Relaxed
Creative	Innovative	Patient	Reliable
Dependable	Intelligent	Perceptive	Reserved
Determined	Introverted	Perfectionist	Resolute
Dignified	Intuitive	Persuasive	Respectful
Disciplined	Jovial	Playful	Responsible

GENERAL TRAITS *(CONTINUED)*

Responsive	Self-Accepting	Spiritual	Witty
Satisfied	Self-Assertive	Useful	Youthful
Scientific	Self-Aware	Warm	
Searching	Sensitive	Wise	

JOB SKILLS

The following is a short list of job skills. (There are literally thousands of job-specific skills.)
You will have to research the job skills specific to your occupation.

Accounting	Drill Press Operation	Scheduling
Auditing	Driving	Soldering
Brake Alignments	Editing	Teaching
Building Maintenance	Electronic Repair	Technical Writing
Carpet Laying	Filing	Telemarketing
Cleaning	Hammering	Typing
Computer Programming	Interviewing	Welding
CNC Machine Operation	Keyboarding	Writing
Composite Engineering	System Administration	Spreadsheet Software
Cooking	Management	Presentation Making Software
Counseling	Mechanical Drafting	Publishing Software
Customer Service	Metal Fabrication	Word Processing Software
Desktop Publishing	Payroll Accounting	Graphic Design Software
Detailing	Public Speaking	Web Design Software

SELF-MANAGEMENT SKILLS

You use self-management skills every day to survive.
Self-management critical and adaptive skills are important
because employers hire people who will fit in with the work group.

———— CRITICAL SKILLS ————

Follow Instructions	Get Things Done	Punctual
Get Along Well with Others	Honest	Responsible

———— ADAPTIVE SKILLS ————

Assertive	Integrity	Self-Motivated
Assume Responsibility	Intelligent	Sense of Direction (Purpose)
Competitive	Inventive	Sense of Humor
Complete Assignments	Kind	Sensitive
Creative	Learn Quickly	Sincere
Decisive	Mature	Sociable
Dependable	Open-Minded	Tactful
Detail-Oriented	Outgoing	Tolerant
Diplomatic	Patient	Tough
Enthusiastic	Persistent	Trusting
Flexible	Physically Strong	Understanding
Friendly	Pleasant	Willing to Learn New Things
Highly Motivated	Proud of Doing a Good Job	
Ingenious	Results-Oriented	

TRANSFERABLE SKILLS

Transferable skills can be transferred from one job or even one career to another.
Critical transferable skills may get you higher levels of responsibility and pay.
Emphasize them in an interview as well as on your resume.

CRITICAL TRANSFERABLE SKILLS

Accept Responsibility	Meet Deadlines	Sales
Budgeting	Project Planning	Supervise Others
Efficiency	Public Speaking	

MECHANICAL SKILLS

Assembling	Grinding	Operating Machines
Balancing, Juggling	Hammering	Physical Agility, Strength
Counting	Hand Crafts	Precise, Tolerance, Standards
Drawing, Painting	Keyboarding, Typing	Restoring
Driving	Keypunching, Drilling	Sandblasting
Endurance	Manual Dexterity	Sewing
Finishing, Refinishing	Modeling, Remodeling	Sorting
Gathering	Observing, Inspecting	Weaving

PEOPLE SKILLS

Caring	Empathy	Mentoring
Comforting	Encouraging	Motivating
Communicating	Group Facilitating	Negotiating
Conflict Management	Helping Others	Outgoing
Conflict Resolution	Inspiring Trust	Problem Solving
Counseling	Inquiry	Respect
Consulting	Instructing	Responsive
Developing Rapport	Interviewing	Sensitive
Diplomacy	Listening	Sympathy
Diversity	Mediating	Tolerance

TRANSFERABLE SKILLS *(CONTINUED)*

DEALING WITH DATA

Analyzing	Cost Analysis	Investigating
Auditing	Counting	Interrelate
Averaging	Detail-Oriented	Organizing
Budgeting	Evaluating	Problem Solving
Calculating, Computing	Examining	Recording Facts
Checking for Accuracy	Financial or Fiscal Analysis	Research
Classifying	Financial Management	Surveying
Comparing	Financial Records	Synthesizing
Compiling	Following Instructions	Taking Inventory

USING WORDS AND IDEAS

Advertising	Imaginative	Quick Thinking
Articulate	Inventive	Sign Language
Brainstorming	Logical	Speech Writing
Correspondence	Promotional Writing	Telephone Skills
Design	Public Speaking	Write Clearly, Concisely
Edit	Publicity	Verbal Communication

LEADERSHIP

Competitive	Integrity	Risk Taker
Coordinating	Judgment	Run Meetings
Decision Making	Manage, Direct Others	Self-Confident
Decisive	Mediate Problems	Self-Directed
Delegate	Motivate People	Self-Motivated
Direct Others	Multitasking	Sets an Example, Sets Pace
Evaluation	Negotiate Agreements	Solve Problems
Goal Setting	Organization	Strategic Planning
Influence Others	Planning	Supervision
Initiate New Tasks	Results-Oriented	Work Schedules

TRANSFERABLE SKILLS *(CONTINUED)*

CREATIVE

Artistic	Illustrating, Sketching	Poetic Images
Dance, Body Movement	Mechanical Drawing	Present Artistic Ideas
Designing	Model-Making	Rendering
Drawing, Painting	Perform	Singing
Expressive	Photography	Visualize Shapes
Handicrafts	Playing a Musical Instrument	Visualizing

OCCUPATIONAL TITLES

Use the following list of job titles as a brainstorming tool when considering job goals.

Accountant	Dentist	Machinist
Administrative Assistant	Doctor	Manager
Architect	Drafter	Mason
Assembler	Editor	Nurse
Cabinet Maker	Engineer	Painter
Carpenter	Financial Analyst	Programmer
Cashier	Graphic Designer	Salesperson
Chef	Inspector	Scientist
Clerk	Lab Technician	Teacher
Cook	Librarian	Veterinarian
Counselor	Machine Operator	Welder

For a more complete list of occupational titles, visit O*Net, www.online.onetcenter.org/, or ISEEK, www.iseek.org/ .

EMPLOYMENT-RELATED TITLES

Community involvement and volunteer experience may be a valuable resource for your job search. Describing your volunteer roles is sometimes challenging, but here's an example of common titles. Just attach the name of the activity or community organization.

Example — YMCA Volunteer or School Fundraiser

Campaigner	Fundraiser	Promoter	Teacher
Consultant	Leader	Secretary	Treasurer
Coordinator	Member	Solicitor	Volunteer
Director	Organizer	Sponsor	Worker

JOB SKILLS IDENTIFICATION

Describe four major tasks you have performed in previous employment that you would like to continue using in your next job. List the skills that were required to perform each task well.

Job Title:

Task _____   Skills _____
_____   _____
                                                          _____
                                                          _____

Task _____   Skills _____
_____   _____
                                                          _____
                                                          _____

Task _____   Skills _____
_____   _____
                                                          _____
                                                          _____

Task _____   Skills _____
_____   _____
                                                          _____
                                                          _____

NOTES

CHAPTER 4

Tools of the Job-Hunting Trade:

Business Cards, Resumes and Cover Letters

"Resume: a written exaggeration of only the good things a person has done in the past, as well as a wish list of the qualities a person would like to have."

— BO BENNETT, WRITER

Before attending a networking group, cold calling a company or answering an ad, you will need a toolkit of marketing materials that tell people who you are and describe your skills and career. In a time of overwhelmed employers and loads of competition, you may need a few versions of the standard toolkit — business cards, resumes, and online or hard copy portfolios — to capture the attention of employers.

The business card is a necessity of networking. Not everyone will want a copy of your resume when you meet them, especially if it's at a professional networking mixer, a social function or even a party at your brother-in-law's home. That's where the business card comes in.

The resume, of course, is the key element of any job search. It will not get you the job, but it may get you in the door. It displays your skills and recaps your professional and personal career. In this chapter, we'll show you how to write a paper resume and a digital resume. We will also provide examples of resumes that have been effective for others.

Providing a portfolio is common for people in advertising, public relations, marketing, journalism, sales and the arts. Portfolios, of course, are adaptable to almost all professions and work well for college students entering the workforce or people returning to the workforce. Just like a resume, a portfolio can take many forms. All portfolios, especially online versions, offer you a richer palette of possibilities for describing your life and career. It's a nice addition to a standard resume and gives you a chance to stretch your creativity in an online environment. More than 90,000 Minnesotans have taken advantage of the eFolioMinnesota, sponsored by Minnesota State Colleges and Universities, and we'll be encouraging you to join them!

Business Cards

Creating business cards is the easiest part of any job search. If you can spell your name and write your contact information correctly, getting a business card together should be a breeze. There are a few ways to make your business card stand out from the pack. When you distribute your business cards at networking events, job fairs or conferences you will want your card to jump out yet leave a favorable impression.

Dave Taylor, an Internet veteran who has published 20 business and technical books and writes the business blog www.intuitive.com, suggests business cards must do three things: 1) supply key contact information, 2) jumpstart recipients' curiosity and 3) jog their memories. Following are some of his suggestions, as well as those of other business card experts.

- Determine the information you want on the card. Of course, you want your name, address, e-mail and phone numbers — work, home and cell phone. If your home phone is shared by your family you might consider adding a second phone number or second line during your search.

- Check for typos. Double- and triple-check your information.

- Give a description of your profession. "Child psychologist," "Web writer and producer," "team leader and machinist," "financial analyst" will give the card recipient at least a small idea of your background and talent. Five or 10 words should take care of it. If you have other certifications or advanced degrees add them after your name but try not to overdo it. The downside is you may look like you're overqualified for many positions; it's a tough call as to when to highlight that information and when to keep it silent.

- Get the cards professionally printed. In a rush? Many copy shops and printers can turn around business cards in hours. Some shops even offer their services online.

- Some people use the back of the business card to list abilities. Some job experts, however, like the idea of leaving that space blank for potential employers to take notes. Like both ideas? You can compromise by listing your attributes on the back but leave room for someone to make a note or two.

- Quality matters. Use thicker card stock rather than cheaper, thinner paper. It tells potential employers you pay attention to small details, like having a business card that does not crumple or tear easily.

Getting Creative With Business Cards

Scott Ginsberg, author of "The Power of Approachability" and writer for the online site www.businessknowhow.com, believes in getting creative with business cards. He's seen business cards of different sizes and shapes, from triangles to circles; some business commentators think 3x5 cards at least break the mold.

He's seen cards with die-cut holes that pop up when open, that contain contact details in Braille and international languages, that carry motivational quotes or that look like baseball trading cards. One Boston banker he knows uses business cards that look like miniature checks.

He has a couple of other simple strategies to remember. Don't forget your cards before leaving home. You never know when you will run into someone who can help in your job search.

If you meet a particularly well-connected individual who seems genuinely interested in helping you land a job, hand her several cards for redistribution to her contacts.

Here are a couple of other good ideas for effective business cards, among them adding a graphic, strong colors or a photo of yourself. Although black and white cards are inexpensive they will not stand out. A colored logo will help add a dash of personality.

A photo, meanwhile, connects you to recipients, reminding them of who you are when they look at their business card collection two weeks or two months after you met. One Minneapolis journalist uses a fun, colorful caricature rendered by a friend who is a cartoonist. Adding color — especially red and black — will help you stand out. A hedge fund manager in Minneapolis once used a black card with white letters simply displaying his website, which drove a remarkable amount of traffic to it from people curious for more information and from potential clients.

Do not overlook the importance of business cards. Certainly, many recipients may toss them into a wastebasket. If even 10 percent put you into a database or a Rolodex you will have made a little headway in your job search.

Resumes

Your resume is an essential part of your job search toolkit. You will need one for whatever kind of job you are looking for. If done properly, it's the document that will move you to a job interview and potential employment.

Do not approach the task of writing the resume lightly. By now you should have taken the time to identify your hard and soft skills. If you cannot identify at least 20 job-related skills at this point, your first task is to revisit Chapter 3 on skills and create a list.

Be aware that your resume is a moving target. Once you have completed one resume you may have to change it frequently to match the qualifications and skills sought by employers for specific jobs. Your resume can be edited, redirected and transformed depending on the jobs you pursue, so having a more general document with adjustable pieces makes sense.

Job seekers start out at different points when preparing resumes. Some will have a resume a few months or a few years old. Others may have been employed for several years and don't have a current resume, or may have one buried on a hard drive they threw out years ago.

Its importance should not be underestimated. "Resume writing is a creative exercise that combines the skills of direct mail with the skills of a storyteller," writes Penelope Trunk in "Brazen Careerist: The New Rules for Success." "You can be great at your job, but unless your current boss is going to personally arrange your next job interview, you're going to have to depend on your resume. Your resume gets you the interview, and you can't get a job without that."

A Four-Step Process

Regardless of where you're starting in writing a resume you should follow a simple four-step process to help you organize your information into a presentable document. First, take a look at resume samples found at WorkForce Centers, online sites, in resume writing books (and this book), as well as from friends and family members. Look at how those resumes are formatted, the language job seekers use and how they describe skills, careers, interests and lives.

Secondly, establish clear objectives for your search. What kind of company do you want to work for? What size? In what field? The same industry you have been in or a different one? What sorts of jobs are you seeking? Answer those questions for yourself and then you can begin to tailor the section of the resume called "job objective."

Now conduct a skills and jobs inventory. Put all your skills together on a sheet and match them as much as possible with your accomplishments as a leader or an employee. Future employers are only marginally interested in the fact you worked for Mega Corporation or DMZ Operations; they want to know what skills you displayed in your work and whether those skills saved money, improved efficiency, led to a more motivated workforce, or whatever. Ask and then answer these questions: What talents have I exercised in my previous positions? How are they relevant to the set of employers I am pursuing?

Trunk, the job search author, encourages you to "list achievements, not job duties ... anyone can do a job, but achievements show you did the job well." A case in point, she writes, is when a job seeker writes: "Managed two people and created a tracking system for marketing." Instead, she says, consider this: "Managed the team that built a tracking system to decrease marketing costs 10 percent." The second example obviously sounds more impressive and leads to a primary goal in resume writing: Always emphasize your achievements in your resume.

Having made an inventory of skills and jobs, you can move on to competencies. What are you good at and what evidence do you have of that? Thinking about competencies is less about listing what you have done and more about your ability to research, work on a team, lead, write, present material before audiences, learn new machinery in a plant environment, or raise a family. This is similar to listing your skills, but focuses instead on skills that have not necessarily been used in jobs. Competencies are exercised skills.

Finally, list all your jobs in a reverse chronological order, with dates of employment and various positions held within various companies. (List your most recent job first, and so forth.) If you have had a rich and varied job career you can list the last three or four jobs and skip your earlier career, or truncate it into single lines: "U.S. Bank, teller, 2000-2005."

Selecting Resume Formats

The five common resume formats are chronological, functional, combination, targeted and keyword. If you're uncertain of which format works best for you, see our Resume Format Comparison Chart at the end of this chapter.

You may end up having an example of each of these formats in your toolbox. The good news is once you have written a decent resume it's easier to go back and customize it for a different employer. You can cut and paste, add and subtract. And by having a relatively simple design, you'll be able to use the same resumes for e-mail attachments, online job seeking sites and snail-mailed submissions. Here's a brief overview of the three approaches.

Chronological

The emphasis for this format is on a chronological listing of employment and employment-related experiences. The format highlights recent employment, while de-emphasizing jobs held years ago. The chronological resume is best for those with a consistent employment history, no gaps in employment and job experiences directly relate to their current goals.

A warning: This may not be the best format for individuals with job gaps, recent graduates or a person changing careers. Those job seekers need to emphasize skills more than work experience.

The chronological approach works well, however, if you have had a steady work record that can be effectively showcased using this format. After topping the resume with your name and contact information — more on that later in this chapter — you list the company, years you worked there (some job seekers use months: "June 2001-present") and a description of your work and accomplishments.

List back previous jobs until you fill a page. If you have had half a dozen jobs over 20 years list at most the last three or four positions and then offer earlier work experience with just the name of employer, your title during that time and dates of employment. For example, "Genetic Corporation, Accounts Payable Associate, 2006-2009."

Moreover, jobs from more than 10 years ago begin to lose impact. If you have valuable experience beyond 10 years, there are ways to present it other than chronologically. Read the following sections on functional and combination resume formats.

Functional

The functional resume highlights skills, experience and accomplishments more than specific dates, names and places. Information is organized by functions or skills that advertise specific qualifications needed for the occupation. This format may work for first-time job seekers and those re-entering the workforce after a gap in employment. Functional resumes allow you to focus more on professional capabilities and much less on chronological achievements.

"The functional resume format is traditionally recommended for first-time job seekers as well as career changers with little or no specific focus," writes Burton Jay Nadler, author of "The Everything Resume Book" and director of the Career Center at the University of Rochester. "Skill summaries tend to be lengthy, presented with the hope that some broadly chosen phrases might stick in the minds of readers and encourage interviews."

Although the goal of this format is to de-emphasize chronological dates, you should still include some employment or volunteer history toward the end of the resume. Failure to include employment or volunteer history could cost you an interview. Including some employment history is better than including none at all.

Combination

The combination resume brings the best of both the chronological and functional resumes. It features a functional section that highlights skills and accomplishments, as well as a chronological listing of employment, education and employment-related experiences. The combination resume is a perhaps the most effective format for many job seekers because it marries your "qualifications" with a list of your past jobs, duties and accomplishments. You can more easily tailor a combination resume to the job you seek.

We have combination resumes at the end of this chapter, as well as worksheets, that will give you a better idea of how the format presents a job seeker's career.

Targeted and Keyword

All resumes should target the needs of a specific occupation. This approach takes it a step further and targets the resume to the specific needs of a specific job. It requires careful research of the employer's needs. Sources of information include company websites, position descriptions, employer profiles, industry publications, networking and informational interviews.

When drafting a targeted resume use keywords and even industry jargon in your resume. This will help you stand out in applicant tracking systems set up to identify the specific skills of applicants. (Applicant tracking systems are software programs an employer uses to identify individuals with certain traits and backgrounds that fit job openings. This allows companies to avoid having to look at hundreds of resumes, many from people poorly qualified for open positions.) Targeted resumes are an absolute necessity for executive positions and specialized technical jobs.

If it's likely the target of your resume is using an applicant tracking system — and the larger the employer, the more likely that will be the case — you should develop a "keyword resume." Critical occupational skills placed at the beginning add impact to the resume and help capture the reader's attention.

The drawbacks of a targeted resume? If a company doesn't have the targeted position available, you may be overlooked. After all, you're applying for a specific job. To avoid this problem use the cover letter to highlight your desire for a specific job yet your openness to being considered for other related openings. That indicates the kind of flexibility many employers seek.

Writing the Resume

A good resume has several visual elements that must be complete and compelling. A few general guidelines exist for showcasing your skills and careers on one or two pages of text. Resumes are fairly predictable in features and information, but some choices have to be made. They are not typically creative documents used to show off your innovative design skills or creative writing skills. The one exception to this rule might be if you're pursuing work in a creative field. Yet even then these resumes must remain cautiously creative.

Now we're going to deconstruct a typical resume, section by section, and even line by line. We'll start at the top, end at the bottom.

Font Selection

There are two types of fonts, serif and sans serif. Serif fonts have tails or feet and sans serif fonts do not. Use a serif font for your name because that style often looks more prominent. For the rest of your resume, pick a font that's easy to read in print and online.

Serif Fonts	Sans Serif Fonts
Baskerville Old	Arial
Bell MT	Helvetica
Bodoni	Century Gothic
Bookman Antiqua	Charlotte Sans
Century	Candara
Garamond	Gill Sans
Georgia	Lucida Sans
Goudy Old Style	Myriad
Times New Roman	Verdana

Name Block

Put your full first name on its own line at the top of the page. Choose your favorite professional-looking font. For ideas, look on the previous page at the list of common, readable fonts that work well for resumes. Your name can be in a different font than the body of the resume. Type your name in bold or CAPITAL LETTERS to make it stand out, and make it larger point type than the body of the resume.

Your address should not contain abbreviations. Include the area code in your landline phone or cell number. It should be a number where you can be reached at all times.

Elizabeth Applicant
1443 HireMe Lane
Employmentville, Minnesota 55555
555-555-5555

Elizabeth.Applicant@fakemail.com

Objective

Include an objective when you are pursuing a specific job goal or when you know the exact title of the position you are applying for. The objective statement, sometimes called a "summary," helps target your resume while limiting its use to those jobs that match your goal. Generally, objectives should be on your resume unless you're applying for a job in your current field and your qualifications are obvious. (You are a nurse, and you're applying for a nursing position, for instance.)

If you choose not to have an objective on your resume page, state one in your cover letter.

If you're applying for a specific job, use the title in your objective and even add the name of the company as in the following example: "Objective: Landscape Design Specialist at Creative Environments Inc."

Here are a few examples of objective statements that clearly indicate precisely what kind of position the job seeker wants.

- Transportation service representative
- Pharmaceutical sales representative
- Office manager
- Senior admissions and enrollment officer

Objective and Summary Statements

A summary statement is a longer version of the objective statement. This option can be used instead of an objective statement. An effective summary statement should sum up your work experience, achievements and skills suited to the position for which you are applying.

The summary should be two to four lines or a series of phrases that may be used in place of the employment objective, or just following it. Here are two examples. One is an objective summary, the other a combination where job hunters boldface the titles of jobs they seek.

Objective: Landscape Architect

Summary: Innovative Landscape Architect with extensive knowledge in construction, engineering and design. Recognized for creatively solving design and sustainability challenges with a positive, customer-focused attitude.

Combination Objective/Summary:

Reliable, caring **Certified Nursing Assistant** with over two years experience caring for elderly and vulnerable adults. Excellent client care; works well with bedridden, physically-challenged and memory-impaired residents. Friendly and compassionate, with excellent interpersonal communication skills. Flexible: available days, evenings, weekends and holidays. Maintains confidential information.

"Qualifications" or "Achievements" Section

Many job seekers using the functional, combination and targeted resumes will feature a section called "skills" or "qualifications." The word "qualifications" does have a certain resonance that "skills" lacks, especially if you are applying for a particular job or in a particular field.

Qualifications don't necessarily have to be all career-related. Your work as a volunteer can be used if it fits into the description of the job you seek. This section should be composed of bullet points no longer than a line or two and no more than four or five in total.

There are two ways to write the qualifications section. One is to call the section "Qualifications" and give a general overview of your skills and career. You might mention you are an experienced presenter, the number of years you have had in a field, your ability to work with others, and any positions you had in which you demonstrated leadership.

A more focused qualifications section might have headlines such as Accounting Qualifications, Consulting Qualifications, Teaching Qualifications. Under these headings you would directly relate your work within that profession, with perhaps a nod to a general skill or two.

In the qualifications section use bullet points — no more than five — and keep the entries to a line or two, at most.

"Achievements" or "Accomplishments"

This is a relatively new idea in resume writing. It probably works better for people in fields like sales, where "achievements" can be more readily quantified. The section can stand on its own or can be added to the "qualifications" section as in "Qualifications and Achievements."

So what goes here? Your ability to grow sales. Your ability to manage people and budgets. Your ability to handle a variety of assignments in your profession. Your experience with software or machines.

Mark Zappa, who works in the Minnesota WorkForce Center in North St. Paul, Minn., calls these "impact statements." They can be located within each job description after you have described your responsibilities. "It can be a summary of your legacy, your best project, your innovations, your work ethic, a huge problem you solved — just about any strength you were known for," he wrote in Career Connection, a publication of the West Metro WorkForce Centers in the Minneapolis region.

It can be an actual testimonial from a supervisor, which he suggests is a nice break from the usual standard resume information. Most jobs can be described to reflect how your talents made for a sparkling performance. In a "non-team" department where everybody took care of themselves, Zappa suggests the impact statement might read: "Identified learning resources and developed productive partnerships within a closed, individual-driven department."

Employment History

List your most recent employment first. A general standard is to list the last three to four jobs or those you have had over the past 10 years, whichever comes first. Focus on recent jobs and your achievements in those positions. Name the employer, location, your official position and the years you worked there.

A constant question is how much information to give about your past jobs. Generally, focus on what you did and your accomplishments during your time in various positions. We offer you a long list of action words to help make your employment history sound more impactful. For example, words such as "maintained, led, worked, performed, developed, directed, established, functioned, monitored and trained" are all examples of action words.

Use bullet points and make your sentences one line. Sentence fragments like "specialized in training new recruits" work fine. Again, list no more than four to six bullet points in describing your last job and then reduce them to two to three points for subsequent positions.

Although contact information is typically given on an application or reference sheet, many resumes still list the employer name, city and state. Other job seekers might limit this information to keep the resume focused on qualifications. The choice is yours. There is no single standard that fits all situations.

Education

If more of your skills and experience come from employment, list employment first and education last. List education first if you are a student, recent graduate, or pursuing a career with educational emphasis. Include the name of the institution, location (city and state), graduation date or projected graduation date, degree(s) earned, field of study and GPA (if over 3.0).

If you haven't been to school in years, you can list education after your professional experience and skip the year you graduated. The reason? You avoid potential and sometimes unconscious age discrimination. Under the education section, you also can have relevant training or certifications that might impress employers or relate specifically to the position you're applying for.

For job seekers who did not graduate from undergraduate or graduate programs a simple disclosure is best: "Attended the University of Minnesota, 1990-1993, Institute of Technology." It shows you have ambition even though you didn't graduate. There may be any number of good reasons why you didn't graduate, so be sure to answer truthfully if an employer asks why a diploma is missing from your wall.

If you never made it to college or finished high school you can list yourself as a high school graduate as long as you have a GED. List the name of the school where you received the GED, or the school district. Do not include an education section if you did not finish high school and had no formal training either in school or from an employer.

Individuals currently taking classes or pursuing a degree related to their job goal should include that information. List the skills acquired, academic accomplishments and the projected date of completion.

Memberships

List organizational memberships related to your job goal. Avoid using non-employer-related or controversial organizations. Stay away from mentioning specific religious or political affiliations or other potentially controversial groups unless they directly relate to the job you want.

Military Experience

Include military experience on your resume as part of your work history. If you are targeting a job within the defense industry, feel free to use military jargon. The defense industry likes candidates who understand the lingo. If you are targeting a job outside of the defense arena, you will need to "civilianize" your military language to show that your skills and experience match the employer's needs.

COMMON TRANSLATIONS

- Infantry = Ground Security Force
- Squad Leader = Team Leader
- NCO = Supervisor/Manager
- Logistics = Warehouse Inventory Control
- Battalion = Division

For more information on communicating military experience to non-military employers, consult the O*Net Online website.

(online.onetcenter.org/)

Volunteer Experience

Featuring volunteer experience can fill in any gaps in employment on a resume. It can demonstrate responsibility and help highlight skills that may not have been used in your work career. Served as an officer of the PTA? Or a coach at your children's school? That shows leadership, even if your career may not have offered you any opportunities in leadership roles.

Hobbies/Personal Interests

Include hobbies and personal interests if they're employment-related, not controversial, and show skills and experience.

References

Do not include your references or the phrase "references available on request" on the actual resume. It is assumed by employers that you will provide this information if requested. Once an employer asks for your references, provide the names of three to five people who can speak favorably about your attributes as an employee and a human being.

Awards/Recognition

Let the employer know of any internal and external awards or recognition you have received (employee of the month, industry awards, and so forth). Those are accomplishments worthy of mention.

Rules of Basic Resume Writing

When writing resumes, there are a few things to keep in mind and a few things to avoid. These are documents meant mainly to get you into an interview with employers by recounting your career and skills in the most economical way possible. Here's a guide on how to craft a strong resume.

Keep It Brief: One to two pages is just about right, unless you are a professor or a doctor.

Focus: Target your job search and your resume to your specific occupational goals.

Prepare Multiple Resumes: Write one well-written resume that targets your immediate job search but be prepared to change it. Or, have another version ready that addresses the needs of other prospective employers. At least two resumes are a necessity for many people, especially those planning to pursue a new occupation.

Provide a Visual Impact: A resume has 10 seconds to convince hiring managers and employers that you should be interviewed, so make it readable. Use white space and bullets. Use indentation.

Check Your Grammar and Spelling: Double and triple check for typographical, grammatical and spelling errors and ask for another set of eyes to proofread it.

Ensure Integrity: Accentuate the positive, skip the negative, be honest.

Target Your Resume: Target resumes to the level of employment, occupation or employer. Make changes to your baseline resume when you're pursuing a different occupation or you're going for a position less advanced than your former job. (This pertains in particular to workers applying for jobs that might pay less than they earned in the past.) Consider taking out information not pertinent to the job you're applying for and add in anything that illustrates the skills that the position requires.

Make It Scannable: Today, you can create a nice resume in Microsoft Word and most employers will be able to scan it. Some job sites, including www. MinnesotaWorks.net, require you send your resume as an RTF file. That's easy. Once you have created your resume in Word or Google docs, or whatever word processing program you're using, open it, go to the "save as" button and save it as an RTF file under a different name. Then open the new resume and remove any lines or computer gibberish that spoils the look of the document.

Print Using Quality Paper: Don't go cheap. Use 24 pound or higher grade, 100 percent cotton fiber paper for a clear, sharp image. White, cream or gray works fine. Avoid colored paper or glossy, high shine finishes. Paper size should be the standard letter size, 8 1/2 x 11.

Make Clear Reproductions: When making copies for distribution, use a laser printer when possible. You can bring your own paper to copy shops, load it in and print while avoiding the extra charge for higher grade paper. Public libraries and WorkForce Centers often have printers available. Test a copy before making dozens of them, and collate correctly.

Get Access to a Computer: Having a computer and Internet connection at home is extremely beneficial to your job search. With netbooks available for as low as $200 you would be wise to make the investment if your budget allows.

If a personal computer does not fit your budget, buy a USB drive, which costs as little as $10, and save your resume on it. Whenever you have access to a computer, you can work on your resume by plugging the drive into a USB port. Otherwise, there are several places to get computer access for free. Computers are available from Minnesota WorkForce Centers, friends and family, schools, social organizations, community agencies, print shops, religious organizations, county human service offices, community action agencies and, of course, public libraries.

The Language of Resumes

Skills statements are a way to effectively communicate your experience and make yourself stand out from other applicants.

One formula goes like this:
Strong Skills Statements = Action Words + Details + Outcome/Result

Choose action verbs that demonstrate responsibility. For example, "managed," "coordinated" or "designed." Vary the action verbs that you choose. This helps make your abilities sound more diverse and adds depth to your resume. Use the list of action verbs provided in this chapter for ideas.

When writing about results take a look back at your recent career and find projects where you participated greatly in a successful delivery of products or services. Tell employers not just about what you did at work, but how you made a positive impact on business operations, productivity on the plant floor or whatever.

THINK CREATIVELY. CONSIDER THESE EXAMPLES OF STRONG SKILLS STATEMENTS:	
Before: Answered phones	**After:** Responded to an average of 200 service inquiry phone calls per day in a helpful and professional manner.
Before: Waited tables	**After:** Managed and maintained eight tables, utilizing interpersonal skills to ensure customer satisfaction through prompt, cordial service.
Before: Drove a truck	**After:** Responsible for ensuring safe and efficient delivery of goods to over 15 vendors while driving a highly sophisticated vehicle.

This information was provided by the University of Minnesota Career and Community Learning Center.

Making the Most of Your Resume

Resumes should be sent to a person by name. Avoid sending the resume to a job title such as "Production Manager." It will take extra effort, but do your research and find out the name and title of the appropriate person to whom your resume should be sent.

If asked send your resume to personnel or human resources. Then also send a resume to the person in charge of the department in which you want to work. Most of the time, personnel does the screening, but it's the department manager who is the final hiring authority.

GENERAL RESUME TIPS

- Lead with your strongest statements that are related to the job or goal.
- Emphasize your skills.
- Keep it brief (one to two pages).
- Use 8 1/2 x 11 paper.
- Correct all typographical, grammatical and spelling errors.
- Include your employment-related accomplishments.
- Target your qualifications.
- Clearly communicate your purpose and value to employers.
- Use the best format to showcase your skills.
- Make your resume relevant to the job.
- Always include a cover letter when mailing your resume.

THINGS TO AVOID

- Using abbreviations (exceptions include middle initial and directions such as "N" for North).
- Using personal pronouns such as "I" to refer to you.
- Mentioning wage history.
- Using fancy typeset, binders or exotic paper.
- Sending a photograph of yourself unless it's relevant (i.e. acting, etc.).
- Making statements that you cannot prove.
- Including personal information (age, height, weight, family status, picture).
- Highlighting religious or political affiliations unless you're applying for a job with one of these organizations.
- Changing the tense of verbs or using the passive voice.
- Using the title "resume."
- Including references on the resume. (Make a separate reference sheet.)
- Including hobbies or social interests unless they contribute to your objective.
- Stapling or folding your resume.
- Using the same action word more than twice.

When mailing your resume, always send it with a cover letter. Mass-mailing your resume to employers does not work. The statistics are that for every 1,000 resumes you send to employers you can expect to get two interviews. Target a smaller pool of employers instead of haphazardly mass mailing to a phone book full of names.

Follow up your resume submissions with a phone call to the employer. Be courteous, professional and persistant about selling your qualifications. Be sure to ask for an interview.

When directly contacting employers, always have a copy of your resume available and take the initiative to offer it to them.

When applying for a job with an employment application, attaching your resume is a good idea. The resume will add impact and should complement the application. If you're asked to fill out an application, never write on it "See resume." Filling out the entire application is still required.

Give a copy of your resume to your references. It provides them with information about you and will help them to talk to an employer about your qualifications.

RESUME STRATEGIES

Once it's done, a resume is like a product. If it sits on a shelf no one will buy it. You have to promote yourself with your resume at networking events, by speaking to potential employers and by submitting it with job applications. Pass it out to the following people:

- Employers with advertised job openings
- Employers with no advertised job openings
- Employment agencies
- Vocational and college placement offices
- Personal and professional networking contacts
- Your references
- Executive recruiters
- Your employment counselors or instructors
- General and niche-based job boards

Hand or send e-mailed copies of your resume to all networking contacts. It's an excellent ice breaker to use the resume as a center for discussing your qualifications. Ask your contacts to critique your resume.

Always bring extra copies of your resume to an interview.

Finally, follow-up, follow-up, follow-up. It's no use mailing resumes if you don't take the time to try to speak to companies directly. The true test of an effective resume is that you're offered interviews. If you aren't getting responses or interviews from your resume, you may want to re-evaluate it.

Cover Letters

Every resume needs to be accompanied by a cover letter. Written in business style, cover letters should contain an expression of your interest in working for a company, an abbreviated introduction to your career and a short, compelling paragraph detailing why you would be a perfect fit for a current or future opening.

Cover letters are not like standard resumes. They cannot be duplicated and sent to several potential employers. Each letter must be targeted for each position you seek or contact you make. Deciding what to put in the letter remains tricky since you do not want to repeat your entire resume, yet you will want to make a strong case for a company to, in fact, look at your skills and experience to see if they fit any open positions.

Cover letters are employed in a variety of circumstances, ranging from applying for advertised jobs to serving as a "letter of introduction" to companies where you want to work, requesting networking leads or informational interviews. The targeted audience may be different, but the general approach remains the same: Put your best foot forward.

Cover Letter Audiences

Cover letters serve different readers. Typically, cover letters are targeted at specific job openings in a company. These "application" letters match your qualifications to a position's advertised requirements.

Another variation, the "prospecting" letter, is used to contact employers who haven't advertised or published job openings. You may have cold-called a company and gotten the name of someone you want to contact with a letter, resume and follow-up call. These letters call for describing your skills and matching them to the perceived needs of the employer based on your research.

The "networking" letter, in contrast, first refers to the person who gave you the referral before asking for an informational interview or, in the case of an opening, consideration for the position. It's fine to ask in a networking letter for recipients to share more contacts at other companies if they're willing.

Whenever using any of these letters remember to include a section attachment — your resume.

Tips for Writing Strong Cover Letters

Cover letters use standard business letter formats. Below your name and address — or masthead — will be the date, followed by an empty line, then the recipient's name and title, street address, city, state and ZIP code.

Address a Person: Always address the letter to a specific person by name and title. Even if responding to a job that states "no phone calls" consider calling to politely ask the name of the hiring authority. You may not always be able to identify the name of a specific person. In this case, send the letter to the title of the recipient (Production Manager, Maintenance Supervisor, Office Manager, Human Resources or Search Committee). Avoid "To Whom It May Concern."

**State Your Intent**: In general, your letter should state your interest in the job. In the case of a letter of introduction, simply state you would like to work for the company. Use the first paragraph to express your energy, enthusiasm, skills, education and work experience that could contribute to the company's success.

Use the second and third paragraphs, or a list of bullet points, that exhibit briefly your talents, experience and achievements. These can be brief summaries of what you illuminate in greater detail in your attached resume.

**The T Formation**: Consider the "T" letter format, which first names the specific requirements an employer has asked for in an ad and your corresponding qualifications. If you have collected a list of likely qualifications for the positions you seek, you can do the same thing.

The strategy might look like the following. An advertised position asks for experience managing, writing, marketing and accounting. You could in the middle section match your skill set to those abilities, as in the following example:

- _**Managing**_: Supervised a department of 10 employees at BS Marketing Inc. in Minneapolis for five years that won three national awards.

- _**Writing**_: Crafted more than 150 brochures and print ads, including several that won awards.

- _**Marketing**_: Led a total of 12 campaigns involving print, Web and radio for three different clients over the past three years.

- _**Accounting**_: Took several financial classes toward an MBA and understand major accounting software systems.

<u>*The Final Paragraph*</u>: Use the final paragraph to mention you will make a follow-up call within a week, perhaps within a few days, to confirm the document has been received and to ask for an interview. Thank the person for taking the time to read your letter. And use the appropriate closing, such as "Sincerely."

<u>*One More Look*</u>: Be sure to proofread your letter to check content, grammar and spelling, and ask someone else to have a look, too. Sign the letter in blue or black ink.

In writing the letters, avoid appearing too familiar, overbearing, humorous or cute. Avoid starting too many sentences or bullet points with "I'" if possible. Keep sentences short and to the point. The entire letter should be one page composed of three to five paragraphs. Remember, your resume will fill in details.

<u>*Mail First Class*</u>: Skip business class envelopes and use 8½ x 11 mailers so you don't have to bother folding your letter and resume. A larger envelope keeps the documents flat and crisp and will be worth the extra cost.

ENDNOTES: Action Words

he following section will be the longest of the book. It contains "action words" and many examples of resumes and cover letters. Even if you are not in the profession represented in the examples, you can certainly borrow the templates, words and techniques offered here.

ACTION WORDS

Use this list of action words to help you create strong skills statements.

Achieved	Awarded	Constructed	Directed
Addressed	Began	Consulted	Distributed
Adjusted	Budgeted	Contacted	Drafted
Administered	Built	Controlled	Earned
Advised	Calculated	Contracted	Edited
Advocated	Catalogued	Convinced	Effected
Affected	Chaired	Converted	Emphasized
Aided	Clarified	Coordinated	Enabled
Analyzed	Coached	Corrected	Encouraged
Applied	Collaborated	Correlated	Enforced
Appointed	Collected	Counseled	Engineered
Appraised	Communicated	Created	Enlarged
Approved	Compared	Customized	Enlisted
Arranged	Compiled	Decided	Equipped
Assembled	Composed	Defined	Established
Assessed	Conceived	Delegated	Estimated
Assigned	Conceptualized	Designed	Evaluated
Assisted	Conserved	Detailed	Examined
Attained	Conducted	Determined	Excelled
Audited	Contributed	Developed	Executed

ACTION WORDS *(CONTINUED)*

Expanded	Increased	Mediated	Searched
Expedited	Influenced	Merged	Secured
Experimented	Informed	Mastered	Selected
Explored	Initiated	Moderated	Simplified
Extracted	Inspected	Modified	Sold
Fabricated	Inspired	Monitored	Solved
Facilitated	Installed	Motivated	Spoke
Familiarized	Instituted	Reduced	Stimulated
Filed	Instructed	Recorded	Streamlined
Focused	Integrated	Recruited	Strengthened
Forecasted	Interacted	Rectified	Structured
Formed	Interpreted	Regulated	Succeeded
Formulated	Interviewed	Rehabilitated	Summarized
Furnished	Introduced	Reinforced	Supplied
Furthered	Invented	Remodeled	Supported
Founded	Investigated	Reorganized	Tailored
Generated	Joined	Repaired	Taught
Governed	Judged	Replaced	Tested
Grouped	Launched	Reported	Tutored
Guided	Lectured	Represented	Transformed
Handled	Led	Researched	Translated
Headed	Located	Resolved	United
Hosted	Logged	Restored	Upgraded
Illustrated	Listened	Reviewed	Utilized
Implemented	Maintained	Revised	Validated
Improved	Managed	Revitalized	Verified
Incorporated	Marketed	Scheduled	

RESUME FORMAT COMPARISON CHART

Format	Characteristic	Advantage	Disadvantage	Use	Don't Use If
Chronological	Presents information in reverse order, most recent experience listed first Offers concise picture of you as a potential employee	Easy to write Emphasizes steady employment record Format is familiar	Calls attention to employment gaps Skills are difficult to spot unless they're listed in the most recent job	To emphasize past career growth and development When continuing in the same career When the name of former employer may be significant to prospective employer	There are gaps in your work history Calling attention to your age could be a problem You've changed jobs often You're entering job market for first time or after a long absence
Functional	Focuses on specific strengths and skills important to employers	Focus on skills, not history De-emphasizes a spotty work history	No detailed work history Content may appear to lack depth May create suspicion you are hiding something	When entering the job market or when reentering after a long absence When work experience has been varied or unrelated When changing careers When primarily consulting or doing freelance work	You want to emphasize growth or development Responsibilities and functions in recent jobs were limited
Combination	All the flexibility and strength of the functional and chronological combined	Shows off a strong employment record with upward mobility Showcases relevant skills and abilities and supportive employment record Emphasizes transferable skills	Work history is often on the second page and employer may not read that far	When shorter functional format would be too sketchy to offer a complete picture of abilities and work history	Experience is limited There are wide gaps in work history
Format Variations					
Keyword	Allows for focused resumes that target skills	Skills are listed briefly and at the beginning of the resume Easy for employer to scan and find skills	May be redundant information to include keywords at the top of your resume Still an unfamiliar format to many employers	For all scannable systems of job screening For new graduates or those reentering the work place or changing careers	There is rarely a time you cannot use this variation. It can be used in combination with any or all of the other formats
Targeted	Highly focused document aimed at a particular job A "capsule" of work experience	Brief and direct Easy to read	May focus too tightly on one particular job Content may appear sparse	When job target is specific When you need separate resumes for different career paths	You aren't prepared to put the effort into writing an excellent resume

OCCUPATIONAL KEYWORDS

Occupational keywords include skills, titles, degrees and occupational buzzwords.

Account Management	Cross-Cultural Training	Journeyman	Raw Materials
Accounts Receivable	Decision Making	Layout Design	Receptionist
Acquisitions	Demographics	Logic Analyzer	Reporter
Bachelor's Degree	Die Casting	Magnetic Theory	Research
Bank Reconciliation	Dietitian	Manager	Sales
Batch Processing	Drywall	Mapping	Secretarial
Benchmarking	Ecology	Marketing	Software Modeling
Blueprint Reading	Electronics	Master's Degree	Spanish
Budget	Employee Assistance	Microprocessor	Spreadsheets
Bulletins	Engineer	Microsoft Word	Stick Welding
CAD	Equipment Vendor	Microsoft Office	Strategic Planning
Calibrator	Facilitator	Nursing	Student Personnel
Carpentry	Financial Planning	Oscillator	Supervisor
Cash Flow	Food Preparation	Patient Advocate	Taxonomy
Cell Culture Media	Gas Pipeline	Payroll	Teacher
Cement	Goal Setting	Personal Computer	Technical Writing
Child Care	Graphic Design	Process Metallurgy	Time Management
Claims Adjudication	Guest Services	Proposal Writing	Transportation
Commercial Leasing	Hiring/Firing	Psychology	Travel
Copy Editing	Hotel	Public Relations	Wave Solder
Counselor	ISO 9000	Purchasing	Workflow
Crisis Management	Journalism	Radio	Writer

Resume Samples

The resume samples on the following pages model the basic formats and principles of resume writing. Consider how each job seeker presents his/her skills and experience. Along with the content, look at how the resume is presented. Draw the best from each to help decide how to style your resume. Ultimately, your resume will be unique to you and won't look exactly like any of these presented.

FUNCTIONAL RESUME

First M. Combotwo

233 2nd Avenue South
Minneapolis, MN 55423

612-123-4567
first_last@yahoo.com

OBJECTIVE

Administrative Assistant IV

SUMMARY

Energetic, self-motivated Administrative Assistant with comprehensive experience in executive level facilities management, sales and marketing support. Creative, flexible and motivated individual with excellent interpersonal communication abilities. Proven organizational and planning expertise; works with minimal supervision. Excellent customer service skills.

QUALIFICATIONS

- Ability to establish and maintain positive client relationships
- Budgeting
- Computer literate. Strong understanding of Microsoft Office, Internet and e-mail applications

- Demonstrated ability to inspire and motivate others
- Enthusiastic self-starter
- Excellent verbal and written communication skills
- Inventory control
- Maintains confidential Information

- Organized with keen attention to detail
- Outcome driven; results oriented
- Problem solver
- Strong interpersonal skills
- Strong work ethic.
- Type over 50 WPM

ACCOMPLISHMENTS

Administrative Support

- Responded to all clerical, scheduling, travel, report generation needs of executive management team, in a timely and efficient manner.
- Managed regional, multiple budgets and expenses for marketing, travel and special events. Consistently met budget constraints.
- Ordered all office supplies and equipment. Negotiated with vendors, ensuring the most cost-effective pricing.

Organizational Skills

- Successfully developed and administered new policies and procedures, effectively reducing employee turnover. Policies were adopted by other regional offices.
- Organized internal communications center to expedite incoming and outgoing correspondence.
- Developed multi-departmental regional facility to centralize purchase and distribution of promotional items, increasing availability and decreasing cost per item.

FUNCTIONAL RESUME *CONTINUED*

COMMUNICATION

- Developed and coordinated software marketing events, successfully increasing customer awareness and product use through hands-on, interactive training.
- Participated in product rollouts, introducing new hardware to targeted market, supporting a team that met and exceeded district sales goals in excess of $103 million annually.
- Coordinated national strategy planning meetings and conferences for both internal and external customers, ensuring that all participants arrived on time, had appropriate accommodations, and positive team experiences.

OPERATIONS / LOGISTICS

- Directed all aspects of office facilities including consulting with corporate staff. This included five successful expansions, downsizing, and relocations of two facilities and 55 people. Ensured personnel needs were met during this transition.
- Recruited, hired and supervised support personnel, ensuring maximum staffing was in place for special projects when needed.
- Evaluated and ordered equipment and sales tools along with approving and processing invoices for all goods and services involving the facility. This resulted in time saving and minimal involvement of staff.

PROFESSIONAL EXPERIENCE

Company	Company	Company	Company
Minnetonka, Minn.	Chanhassen, Minn.	New Hope, Minn.	Bloomington, Minn.
2000–2004	1998–2000	1991–1998	1990–1991
Title	Title	Title	Title

RECOGNITIONS AND AWARDS

Recognized as "Support Team Member of the Year"

Won "Contributor of the Quarter Award" three times in 2½ years

Winner of the "Impact" award for facilities management

TARGETED RESUME: PROFESSIONAL IN HEALTH CARE

First Last

111 South Street #101
Minneapolis, Minnesota 55407

612.821.0000

SUMMARY

Reliable, caring Certified Nursing Assistant with over two years experience caring for elderly and vulnerable adults. Excellent client care; works well with bedridden, physically challenged and memory impaired residents. Friendly and compassionate, with excellent interpersonal communication skills. Flexible: available days, evenings, weekends and holidays. Maintains confidential information.

LICENSES and CERTIFICATIONS

- Minnesota CNA License in good standing
- CPR certified

QUALIFICATIONS

- Assist individuals with meals as needed
- Helps patients with personal hygiene
- Comforts and motivates patients
- Manages pericare routine and clean-up for coroner

- Complies with OSHA and HIPPA regulations
- Positive attitude
- Ensures resident rooms are neat
- Reacts quickly in emergency situations

- Excellent attendance record
- Will pass physical and TB tests
- Follows direction of nurses
- Works with minimal supervision

ACCOMPLISHMENTS
Communication:

- Offered conversation and companionship to long-term care residents, establishing and maintaining positive patient relationships.
- Responded to patient calls in a timely and efficient manner. Determined need and provided for care of individuals.

- Related well with team members, residents and families.
- Provided social and emotional support; encouraged residents who felt sad or lonely.
- Observed physical and emotional changes; reported patient conditions to nurses.

TARGETED RESUME: PROFESSIONAL IN HEALTH CARE *CONTINUED*

ACCOMPLISHMENTS continued

Care and Support:

- Assisted residents in the process of getting ready for the day; ensured they were comfortably on time for all meals and activities.

- Helped residents with daily hygiene including showering, oral and pericare, incontinence care, minimizing rashes, sores and soiling.

- Aided residents with dressing.

- Transferred individuals from bed to chair, bed to commode, chair to commode, using Gait Belts, Hoyer Lifts and EasyStands as needed, ensuring patient safety and comfort.

- Treated residents with respect and dignity.

Organizational Skills:

- Visited with and evaluated patients daily to determine which patients needed more time to prepare for the day and to respect the needs of each individual.

- Inventoried housekeeping and personal supplies of residents. Replaced or had supplies ordered as needed.

Activities:

- Supported and helped residents with field trips, arts and crafts, music, games and reading activities. Ensured participants arrived on time, had needed accommodations and positive experiences.

- Worked range of motion activities with patients as instructed by LPN or RN.

- Helped patients with daily living activities including walking and exercising; helped residents achieve a good quality of life.

PROFESSIONAL EXPERIENCE

Certified Nursing Assistant	Certified Nursing Assistant	Certified Nursing Assistant
Reliable Residential Care	Lutheran Care Center	MCTC
St. Paul, Minn.	That Town, Minn.	Minneapolis, Minn.
2004 – 2006	2006 – 2007	2008

EDUCATION

High School Graduate
Your High School
Your City, Ill.

CHRONOLOGICAL — SKILLS

First M. Chronological
012 Your Avenue South # 345
Minneapolis, MN 55418
612.123.4567
firstmchronological@yahoo.com

SUMMARY—

Innovative, enthusiastic Transportation Service Representative with extensive experience in billing, sales and client service operations. Dynamic, goal-oriented, highly skilled and flexible. Dedicated to meeting or exceeding internal and external customer requirements.

RELATED SKILLS AND ABILITIES—

- Account management
- Keyboard over 25 words per minute, 10 - key
- Motivated, client-focused
- Call center experience
- Multitask in fast-paced environment
- Computer and Internet proficient
- Quality customer service
- Document processing
- Service center liaison
- Excellent data and order entry skills
- Timely, accurate
- Extensive billing experience
- Trouble shooting and problem solving

WORK EXPERIENCE—

COMPANY NAME
Customer Service / Night Auditor
Minneapolis, Minn.
612.123.4567

- Accurately and efficiently organize and run nightly audit reports, identifying and correcting all discrepancies.

- Answer phone system, assist visitors with check in and checkout procedures, and respond to all guest inquiries in a timely, professional manner.

- Maintain contact with various internal departments and external entities to prevent, minimize or resolve service problems involving or related to customers.

CHRONOLOGICAL — SKILLS *CONTINUED*

WORK EXPERIENCE—
(continued)

COMPANY NAME
Leasing Agent
Minneapolis, Minn.
612.123.4567

- Showed and leased apartments to prospective tenants, professionally demonstrating proficient communication and negotiation skills.

- Obtained credit reports, ensuring that prospective tenants met business criteria; reduced the write-off of bad debt.

COMPANY NAME
Administrative Assistant
Minneapolis, Minn.
612.123.4567

- Provided quality administrative support allowing marketing reps to meet their sales goals.

- Created and generated business billing, resolving problems and facilitating corrections to maintain corporate revenues and assure customer satisfaction.

COMPANY NAME
Customer Service Representative
Edina, Minn.
612.123.4567

- Supported the prompt delivery of telecommunication services by providing internal and external customers with timely, accurate information.

- Identified customers' needs; investigated and corrected chronic service problems.

EDUCATION—

AA
Business Computer Training Institute, Seattle, Wash.

Molly McGinnis

18881 NoName Trail, Lakeville, MN 55044
952-000-0000
mollyk.mcginnis@ymail.com

Skilled and dedicated professional with years of experience in the medical/legal field. Demonstrated capacity to provide comprehensive support; excel at problem solving, resolution and managing daily tasks. Proven track record of accurately completing and managing files with demanding deadlines.

— KEY QUALIFICATIONS INCLUDE —

- Document Management/Filing
- Pharmaceutical Management
- Personal Injury
- Chart Summaries
- Drafting Legal Documents

- Discovery
- Research
- Workers Compensation
- Editing/Proofreading
- Inter-Department Communications
- Litigation

- Transcription
- Client Relations
- Resolution
- Quality Assurance
- Paralegal
- Medical DME
- Medical Assistant

— SOLID TECHNICAL ABILITIES —

Microsoft Office, Excel, PC Law, Transcription, Access,
Power Point, Internet/e-mail, 75 wpm typing

— RELEVANT EXPERIENCE —

LAW FIRM,	MINNEAPOLIS, MINN.	09/09–11/09

Family Law, Real Estate, Probate Paralegal/Temporary Assignment

- Created accurate professional memos, letters and legal documents. Proficient in the chronological order of chart summaries. Maintained client files and correspondence. Responsible for calendaring client court dates. Scheduled client/attorney conferences. Answered incoming telephone calls/distributed accurate messages, and maintained client informational updates.

LAW FIRM,	ST. PAUL, MINN.	12/08–5/09

Leasing/Paralegal/Temporary Assignment

- Managed/distributed leasing documents via photocopy, fax, FedEx, internal/external mail, messenger service and e-mail; maintained files. Typed and processed legal documents for court filings/legal pleadings. Created and maintained all commercial real estate lease contracts. Obtained background record research. Created tracking spreadsheet for A/R invoicing and collections. Provided community resources.

SKILLS AND CHRONOLOGICAL *CONTINUED*

— RELEVANT EXPERIENCE —
CONTINUED

LAW FIRM,	**MINNEAPOLIS, MINN.**	**10/07–7/08**

Mortgage Foreclosure Paralegal

- Created accurate professional memos, letters and legal correspondence for foreclosures.
- Communicated with real estate agents and clients on status of foreclosure five-week redemption process. Implemented and created an Excel spreadsheet to track real estate affidavits sent and received. Created client invoices. Drafted legal foreclosure documents. Awarded employee achievement for developing tracking system for abandonment affidavits.

**TEMPORARY CONTRACT ASSIGNMENTS,
MINNEAPOLIS, MINN.**   **6/06–5/07**

Medical/Legal

Regis— Responsible for drafting and editing of commercial franchise contracts, estoppels/SNDA. Assisted clients with franchise process.

Law Firm— Created accurate professional memos, letters and legal documents. Proficient in the chronological order of chart summaries. Maintained client files and correspondence.

Hennepin County— Supervised and facilitated training on dictation system. Responsible for downloading of transcription into dictation system. Assisted departmental programs for legal, medical and community awareness.

— EDUCATION AND PROFESSIONAL DEVELOPMENT —

Associate in Applied Science, Paralegal
• Minnesota School of Business • Richfield, Minn.•
• Honors • GPA 3.63 •

Associate in Applied Science, Medical Assistant
• Eaton College of Business • San Diego, Calif. •

Insurance/Collection Certified, Insurance Collection Specialist
• McAvery Associates • San Diego, Calif. •

Law Firm
• Paralegal Internship • 6/07–8/07 •

Mortgage foreclosure pre-sale process of files,
preparation of affidavits, legal pleadings, summons and complaints,
review of legal documents for court filing, bankruptcy, processed invoices.

CAREER PROFILE-CHRONOLOGICAL

Corrine Casanova

123 Filed St. NE • Blaine, Minnesota 55434
casanovacorrine@msmn.com • 612.123.4567

CAREER PROFILE

I am a creative, efficient, persuasive, deadline-driven client-focused writer, editor and project manager with a passion for health and wellness. My skills include project management, writing of print and web content, substantive editing, copyediting, proofreading, medical writing, acquisitions, contract negotiation, video production, research, analysis, public speaking, marketing

EXPERIENCE

PARK NICOLLET, HEALTH SERVICES • ST. LOUIS PARK, MINN. • 2007-2009

Park Nicollet is an integrated care system that includes Methodist Hospital, Park Nicollet Clinic, Park Nicollet Foundation and Park Nicollet Institute.

HEALTH EDUCATION WRITER • HEALTH EDUCATION • 2008–2009

- Coordinated and developed patient education materials and web content for Methodist Hospital and various Park Nicollet clinics.
- Collaborated with physicians and other clinical professionals to create a strategy for delivering high quality patient education programs using needs assessment tools.
- Compiled, wrote and edited patient education materials with internal clinical experts in the areas of bariatric surgery, eating disorders and pediatric obesity to create customizable patient binders allowing patients to have all their needed materials in one location.

DEVELOPMENTAL EDITOR • INTERNATIONAL DIABETES CENTER • 2007-2008

- Planned and developed high-quality diabetes education publications.
- Effectively led project development teams by creating and nurturing a strong team atmosphere with clinical partners.
- Communicated complex health and scientific concepts to patients written in a fifth grade reading level or below.
- Marketed services at national diabetes educator conferences.

HAZELDEN FOUNDATION, PUBLISHING & EDUCATION • CENTER CITY, MINN. • 1998-2007

Hazelden is a private not-for-profit alcohol and drug addiction treatment center. The Publishing & Education division provides proven-effective research based educational materials to professionals and clients in a variety of institutional settings.

ACQUISITIONS EDITOR/VIDEO PRODUCER
CRIMINAL JUSTICE/CHEMICAL DEPENDENCY TREATMENT TEAM • 2002-2007

- Acquired, developed and edited research-based curricula pertaining to substance abuse/ dependence in a treatment center, health care and criminal justice setting.
- Played a leading role in developing publishing strategy and ensuring the publication of curricula to meet a $5 million net revenue goal.

CAREER PROFILE-CHRONOLOGICAL *CONTINUED*

HAZELDEN FOUNDATION *(continued)*

- Completed profit and loss statements and consistently met budget requirements.
- Regularly reviewed research- and evidence-based practices in the areas of criminal justice and chemical dependency treatment.
- Hired and supervised freelance writers, editors and video production companies.
- Actively pursued project acquisitions at national/international conferences.
- Worked closely with authors, marketers and copy editors from manuscript development through publication.
- Negotiated contracts with authors, attorneys, government agencies and literary agents.
- Handled all managerial tasks in addition to regular job duties during supervisor's nine-month leave of absence.

ACQUISITIONS EDITOR
CHRONIC ILLNESS INITIATIVE/HEALTHY LIVING RESOURCES • 1998-2001

- Acquired, developed and edited self-help and health care books for trade market.
- Developed and edited trade and professional books, video scripts and curricula.
- Coordinated public events for organization's 50th anniversary celebration.
- Evaluated trade proposals for publication.
- Approved marketing copy prior to publication.

UNIVERSITY OF MINNESOTA • MINNEAPOLIS, MINN. • 1988-1998
The University of Minnesota is a public research university.

MANAGING EDITOR • JOURNAL OF AGRICULTURAL & FOOD CHEMISTRY
AMERICAN CHEMICAL SOCIETY • 1996-1998

ASSISTANT TO THE EDITOR • JOURNAL OF DENTAL RESEARCH
INTERNATIONAL ASSOCIATION OF DENTAL RESEARCH • 1993-1996

ASSISTANT TO THE DIRECTOR • DENTAL RESEARCH INSTITUTE • 1988-1993

EDUCATION
BACHELOR OF ARTS • JOURNALISM/NEWS-EDITORIAL SEQUENCE
UNIVERSITY OF MINNESOTA, MINNEAPOLIS, MINN.

ACCOMPLISHMENTS

- Lead and coordinator, Run Club, Coon Rapids Life Time Fitness, 2006-present
- Certified Toastmaster, Toastmasters International, 2007
- Freelance writer, published three articles in national magazine, *Today's Health & Wellness*
- American Council on Exercise group fitness instructor certification (in progress)

SUMMARY RESUME

Brian M. Roggow

612 North 8th Street, St. Peter, MN 56082
Brian.Roggow@mchsi.com • (507) 123-4567
Seeking a position in the capacity of:
Supply Chain Manager

CAREER OBJECTIVE

Procure a position in the supply chain field while utilizing numerous years of experience in many aspects of a manufacturing environment. Work in an atmosphere where continuous improvement, employee development, dedication, creativity, mentoring, policy and procedure enforcement are encouraged in a team environment.

RESUME SUMMARY

Hands-on professional with 20+ years experience in high volume purchasing ($18 million buy in 2008), domestic and global supply chain management, purchasing management, inventory control, production planning, warehouse management, transportation and plant management in an ISO 9001 environment.

Experienced with raw and finished commodities including bulk candy, office supplies, and aluminum castings. Customers have included industry leaders such as Wal-Mart, Target, Menards, John Deere, Toro, G.E. Medical.

Proficient use of Microsoft Word, Outlook, Excel and MRP manufacturing softwares.

Specific strengths includes: total cost analysis, domestic and international supply chain purchasing, internal procedure analysis, strong MRP and ERP procedural knowledge, excellent ERP software navigation, MRP requisition/PO process implementation, conflict resolution, design and implementation of supplier agreements.

Highly experienced in ABC inventory analysis, warehouse storage capacity analysis and design, Lean manufacturing concepts and transportation systems.

INDUSTRY-RELATED EXPERIENCE

EMERSON NETWORK POWER
Waseca, Minn. 12-09 to spring 2010

Currently employed in a three-month contract to hire position as one of several Senior Buyer/Expediters.

Hired to hit the ground running utilizing all past purchasing experience listed above for a facility that is undergoing a two-division consolidation coupled with total migration of old to new ERP software.

Daily use of MRP and discrete shortage reports driving on the spot high dollar purchasing while expediting production floor shortages.

Daily input to Divisional Supply Chain Director concerning improper purchasing practices.

Working with Emerson internal global supply chain purchasing products from China and Mexico.

LOU-RICH INC.
Albert Lea, Minn. 12-07 to 5-09 permanent layoff

Buyer of domestic and foreign metal casting commodities for ISO 9001 contract manufacturer.

Personally responsible for 2008 purchases exceeding $18 million.

Executed corporate and strategic plans to meet goals, including commodity price reductions, forecast product purchasing, supplier consolidation, supplier and part certification, physical inventory elimination and maintenance, on-time delivery performance and inventory turns

Introduced a custom MRP Software Crystal Report to Purchasing management designed to isolate item

SUMMARY RESUME *CONTINUED*

LOU-RICH INC. *(continued)*

purchase pricing discrepancies. This report assisted in recognizing a $57K annual savings from one supplier for one SKU during the first three months of employment.

Introduced EOQ Spreadsheet to management staff, which was adopted as a departmental guide and used by four other department buyers within the organization.

Led troubleshooting effort to resolve receiving and A/P issues, working with supplier and internal receiving and finance departments.

LINDSAY WINDOW
Mankato, Minn., 4-95 to 2-07

Supply Chain Manager — My primary direct responsibilities were all supply chain activities including production and capacity planning, all purchasing and inventory related functions, daily input to production floor management and customer service while supervising warehouse and shipping activities.

Implemented supply chain techniques focusing on annual company spending, supply market, total cost analysis, identification of suitable suppliers, and development of sourcing strategies while minimizing risk and costs.

LINDSAY WINDOW *(continued)*

Developed and maintained all supplier files and confidential purchase agreements.

Provided daily work assignments and production priorities to departmental supervisors and employees.

SHARI CANDIES
Mankato, Minn., 11-73 to 11-87,
company went out of business

Employed in progressive roles in warehouse, promoted to inventory control manager and then promoted to production and transportation manager.

Developed perpetual inventory system of raw materials to provide accurate daily/monthly inventory levels and unit sales data.

Developed and implemented MRP system for controlling inventories of finished product. Production supervisor utilized this information to maximize production and minimize outages.

Promoted to production and transportation manager with primary responsibility for freight and production departments.

Purchased all packaging materials ranging from corrugated boxes, label stock, pallets and several types of poly bags.

OTHER EXPERIENCE

TC Construction — St. Peter, Minn., 4-93 to 5-95 — Carpenter; new construction home framer in Minneapolis

Scheels Sport Shop — Mankato, Minn., 10-89 to 4-93 — Customer service manager

TC Construction — St. Peter, Minn., 3-88 to 10-89 — Carpenter; new construction home framer in Minneapolis

EDUCATION

Currently enrolled in APICS CPIM certification classes with projected completion date of 2-1-2010. Some college courses. On-the-job training, experience and management mentoring coupled with educational seminars/conferences with topics ranging from project and time management to vendor negotiation skills, supervisory training, Lean concepts and personal development courses have provided the bulk of my pertinent education. This experience, combined with a strong work ethic, excellent problem-solving and organizational skills, a strong manufacturing background, and a keen sense of analysis, has allowed me to rise quickly into management roles. I stay current with industry trends and the global business environment by reading purchasing and supply chain management publications.

SCHOOL-TO-WORK CHRONOLOGICAL

ELIZABETH JONES

000 Ames Drive • Eden Prairie, Minnesota 55347
(952) 123-4567 • jones@umn.edu

OBJECTIVE

A public relations position using my skills in writing,
graphic design, web design, marketing and social media.

SKILLS

Promotion: Twin Cities label representative for Chicago-based
Aware Records.

Media: Interned with two corporations writing press releases
and helping develop marketing strategies.

Social Media: Created, promoted and provided content for a
blog focused on the local music scene.

Research: Keen understanding of pop culture, current pop
issues and evolving trends.

EMPLOYMENT HISTORY

Compellent Technologies
June 2008 – September 2009
Research Intern, Marketing Intern

Best Buy
January 2006 – November 2006
Media Sales Associate

WORK RELATED EXPERIENCE

Come Pick Me Up
January 2006 – Present
www.comepickmeup.net
Creator, Writer, Developer
Live show reviews, new band features, music news.

Aware Records
Chicago, Illinois
Summer 2001– Present
Label Rep — Responsible for marketing a roster of music artist and Aware products by using a variety of materials for both grassroots marketing and online promotions.

AjiSignal.com
August 2007 – December 2007
Staff Writer — Wrote weekly articles, such as new band features or show reviews, about music related happenings in the Twin Cities.

The Music, The Message
February 2006 – January 2008
(formerly EmotionalPunk.com)
Staff Writer — Reviewed records, conducted band interviews with both major label and independent artists, live show reviews.

EDUCATION

University of Minnesota
Minneapolis, Minn.
September 2006 – May 2009
Bachelor of Arts
School of Journalism and Mass Communication
GPA: 3.81

University of St. Thomas
St. Paul, Minn.
September 2005 – May 2006
GPA: 3.93

City University
London, United Kingdom

University of Westminster
London, United Kingdom

Cover Letter Formats

$\mathcal{M}$any employers will first ask you to fill out an application and submit a resume. While the cover letter may have diminished somewhat in importance, it does not mean you shouldn't take the care to write a good one. Here is an overview and a few of examples of cover letters.

GENERAL OUTLINE

Your Name
Street Address
City, State Zip Code
Phone Number
E-mail Address

Date

Individual's Name
Job Title
Name of Organization
Street Address
City, State Zip Code

Dear Mr./Ms. Employer:

First Paragraph: State the reason for writing. Name the specific position or type of work for which you're applying. Mention how you learned of the opening.

Second Paragraph: Explain why you're interested in working for this employer and specify how you're PERFECT for this position. Don't repeat the information on your resume. Include something special or unique about yourself that will benefit the employer. Remember, the reader will consider this an example of your writing skills.

Third Paragraph: Mention your resume is enclosed and indicate your desire to meet with the employer. You may want to suggest alternate dates and times, or simply advise them of your flexibility to the time and place. Include contact information where you can be easily reached. Include a statement or question that will encourage the reader to respond. Be sure to communicate your plan to follow up. Finally, thank the employer for his/her time.

Sincerely,

(Your signature in blue or black ink)
Your typed name

Enclosure

"T" COVER LETTER FORMAT

Molly McGinnis
18881 No Name Trail, Lakeville, MN 55044
(952) 123-4567, molly.mcginnis@ymail.com

January 4, 2010

Travelers Insurance
Human Resource Department
One Tower Square
Hartford, CT 06183

Dear Human Resource:

I am very interested in the open Workers Compensation Case Manager position located in St. Paul, Minn., advertised on your company website on January 4, 2010. Having related experience in the medical, legal and business industry makes me a qualified candidate for your needs.

Your Needs	My Qualifications
• Workers compensation experience	• High volume workers compensation claims
• Management of files	• File management/ case management
• Claim resolution	• Handled resolution 150+ files
• Negotiation/settlements	• Evaluation of claim settlement

To aid your efforts in qualifying possible candidates, I have attached a detailed resume for your review. I am confident you will find my background and experience an excellent match for the talents you are seeking. I welcome the opportunity to speak with you in person about my qualifications and look forward to your response. Thank you for your consideration.

Sincerely,

Molly McGinnis
Encl.

COVER LETTER FOR POSTED JOB

Corrine Casanova
10936 Fillmore St. NE • Blaine, Minnesota 55434 • 612.123.4567
casanova_277@msn.com

December 22, 2010

Minnesota Historical Society
Human Resources Department
345 Kellogg Blvd. W.
St. Paul, MN 55102

Dear human resources representative,

I am very interested in the position of Editor and creating the Minnesota encyclopedia. You indicated you were looking for someone with the ability to:

- **Coordinate project activities of encyclopedia of Minnesota**
  As a former acquisitions editor, I have coordinated all aspects of book publishing from idea inception to publication.

- **Perform substantive editing on content**
  I have over nine years of substantive editing experience in book publishing.

- **Develop professional relationships with colleagues, authors, publishers, etc.**
  I have a proven track record of developing relationships with professionals and negotiating publishing agreements.

- **Organize own time well, coordinate multiple projects**
  I am self-motivated and have consistently juggled and managed effectively three to four projects simultaneously.

I have what it takes to create an encyclopedia of Minnesota on time and on budget. I am an excellent candidate for this position and would welcome an opportunity to discuss my skills in person. I love Minnesota history as much as a cold glass of creamy eggnog during the holidays! Thank you for your consideration.

Sincerely,

Corrine Casanova
Enclosure

COLD-CONTACT COVER LETTER

Karen Kareer
5555 Lakewood Road
Somewhere, MN 55555
(555) 555-5555
kkareer@fakemail.com

May 20, 2010

Ms. Francisca Favor
Department Manager
EFTG Industries, Inc.
210 Industry Avenue
Anytown, MN 55555

Dear Ms. Favor:

As you know, innovation and new ways of thinking are important to a company's success. With my history of marketing achievement, I have proven to be an excellent communicator as well as a valuable innovator. This letter is in regard to my strong interest in your company and my desire to contribute to its success.

Presently, I am marketing computer products for a major supplier using online, television and news advertising. My supervisors have commended me for finding creative ways to spend less money and receive greater return.

Enclosed is my resume for your review and consideration. EFTG Industries has a reputation for excellence. I would like the opportunity to use my talents to market your quality line of technical products. I will call you to further discuss my qualifications and how I can benefit your company. If you prefer, you may reach me in the evenings at (555) 555-5555.

Thank you for your time. I look forward to meeting you.

Sincerely,

Karen Kareer

Enclosure

INVITED COVER LETTER

Johnny Network
5555 Lakewood Road
Somewhere, MN 55555
(555) 555-5555
Johnny.Network@fakemail.com

June 26, 2010

Mr. Phillip Morework
Production Manager
XYZ Corporation
21 Industry Lane
Anytown, MN 55555

Dear Mr. Morework:

Please consider my qualifications for the Lead Production Assistant opportunity, which was posted on your website on June 20, 2010. With a proven high-tech background in Fortune 100 companies, I am well qualified and eager to represent your company in this capacity.

Environments that are fast paced, require multi-tasking and value production deadlines are where I thrive. In relation to leadership, I have been responsible for up to 35 staff members and have built a reputation for making quality administrative decisions in a fair and consistent manner. Constant negotiations with all levels of management and staff have strengthened my interpersonal skills.

Enclosed is my resume, and I am looking forward to discussing my potential with you. I will call you to confirm receipt of this information and to discuss possible next steps. Thank you very much for your time and consideration.

Sincerely,

Johnny Network

Enclosure

INVITED COVER LETTER — NO PAID-WORK EXPERIENCE

Wanda Job
5555 Lakewood Road
Somewhere, MN 55555
(555) 555-5555
wandajob@fakemail.com

January 6, 2010

Ms. Marilyn Payer
Housekeeping Manager
Rodetown Inn
123 Indiana Drive
Anytown, MN 55555

Dear Ms. Payer:

Your ad for a Housekeeper in the Jobs Now newspaper on Sunday, January 4, 2010, caught my attention. With over 15 years of housekeeping and home maintenance experience, I believe that I have the necessary skills for the position. My resume is enclosed for your consideration.

Rodetown Inn has an excellent reputation in the community as a quality employer, and my skills perfectly match the requirements. Having been a homeowner for more than five years, I do all of my own maintenance and repair. For the past three years I have been a home care volunteer for the Salvation Army's "Be Friends" program. This includes helping disabled and elderly persons with household chores such as: bed-making, cleaning, vacuuming, dusting, doing laundry, washing walls and windows, mopping, mowing, raking and shoveling. Several patrons have commended me for being extremely reliable, efficient, organized and a good team worker.

This opportunity to apply my skills in a new environment is exciting to me. It would be beneficial for us to meet to discuss the position and my qualifications in greater detail. I will contact you to determine when a convenient interview time might be arranged. Please feel free to contact me in the interim at the number shown above. Thank you for your time. I look forward to talking with you soon.

Sincerely,

Wanda Job
Enclosure

REFERRAL COVER LETTER

Susan Jones
5555 Lakewood Road
Somewhere, MN 55555
(555) 555-5555
SJones@fakemail.com

July 31, 2010

Ms. Rhonda Leland
Corporate Manager
Doneright Corporation
42 Industry Circle
Somewhere Else, MN 55555

Dear Ms. Leland:

Mary Smith, Vice President of Marketing with Doneright Corporation, suggested that I contact you directly regarding my interest in an Administrative Assistant position with your organization. Although my resume is actively on file in Human Resources, Ms. Smith felt that you would want to be made aware of my unique qualifications and availability. Enclosed is a copy of my resume for your consideration.

My solid background makes me a highly qualified Administrative Assistant. With more than four years of experience in executive management for a large manufacturing company, I have mastered the skills necessary to succeed at Doneright. My qualifications include extensive PC experience with the software used at Doneright Corp. (PowerPoint, Excel and MS Office), proven customer service skills, itinerary planning and report writing.

I will be in your area on August 20, 2010, between 9 a.m. and 3 p.m., and would appreciate an opportunity to meet with you to discuss my qualifications in greater detail. I plan to contact you to arrange a possible meeting time.

Thank you for your time and consideration.

Sincerely,

Susan Jones

Enclosure

c: M. Smith

JOB MATCH COVER LETTER

Your Name
Address
City, State, Zip Code
Phone Number
E-mail Address

February 25, 2010

Ms. Jane Smith, Title
Work Incorporated
555 Pine Street
St. Paul, MN 55555

Dear Ms. Smith:

The position of Administrative Assistant listed in the Daily Tribune on February 24, 2010, caught my attention. The skills and qualifications you require closely match my experience in this career field.

- *Detail-oriented, experienced Administrative Assistant:*
  Four years Administrative Assistant experience with responsibility for numerous detailed reports.

- *Assist Customer Relations Manager:*
  Worked with our Customer Relations Manager for two years.

- *Corporate experience with major clients:*
  Regularly served purchasing agents at Fortune 500 companies.

- *PC knowledge:*
  Mastery of the entire Microsoft Office suite.

Enclosed is my resume for your review and consideration. I believe I am an excellent candidate for this position and look forward to meeting with you to discuss it in greater detail. I will plan to call you to determine when an interview might be possible. Thank you.

Sincerely,

(Signature)
Typed Name

Enclosure

CHAPTER 5

Applications, References and Portfolios

"The closest to perfection a person ever comes is when he fills out a job application form."

— STANLEY J. RANDALL, WRITER

A necessary part of every job pursuit is the job application. It's an online or paper form requiring you to fill out information illustrating your career, education and qualifications. It can be a tedious process without the right preparation because it requires a great deal of detail, from dates of employment to addresses and supervisors. Correctly completing an application should not be underestimated since some employers require you to submit one before they will look at your resume or cover letter.

Applications will be studied and compared with other job seekers by human resource personnel, hiring managers, division heads and, at larger companies, applicant tracking software. The document provides another opportunity to sell yourself to potential employers and offer a good first impression.

Online job applications are popular with employers because they are easier to manage. Many employers will ask you to complete an application prior to their staffs even glancing at your resume or cover letter. Why? When several people apply for the same position employers can pre-screen applicants by using automated assessments done by applicant tracking software.

Guidelines for Applications

Applications are a big part of every job seeker's life. Many online job sites require you to complete an application that can be reused frequently as you apply for jobs. At some point companies you have targeted will want you to fill one out. And they require a lot of details: personal information, dates of previous jobs, former supervisors, reasons for leaving jobs and skills you have developed throughout your career.

Creating a Personal Data Record

Several strategies can help shorten the time required to complete applications. Once you have the basic information collected, you only have to repurpose it again — and again and again. Start by creating a Personal Data Record. This will have your job career history and personal information in an online or paper file.

Preferably, you should have your data record as a digital file because you can then simply cut and paste the information into applications as you fill them out. Another time-saving device is the "auto-fill" feature available on Firefox and as part of Google's toolbar. The built-in function allows you to fill out personal data once and then have it automatically populate online applications and other Web-based forms.

So, what information do you need for standard issue applications?

Obviously, be ready with your name, address, phone numbers (business, home, fax and mobile) and e-mail address. Then, collect your career information — your past four jobs (or more or less), the addresses and phone numbers of those companies, your managers in each of those positions and their phone numbers.

TIPS FOR COMPLETING AN APPLICATION

- Never use abbreviations, slang or emoticons (those online symbols for a person's mood or expression).

- Refrain from writing "see resume" on sites requesting that you attach a resume since applicant tracking systems may not understand that phrase. Fill out the entire application.

- For paper applications keep your cheat sheet — the Personal Data Record you created — available so you avoid making errors. Print clearly in black ink, do not use abbreviations and respond to all questions. Use N/A (not applicable) if the section does not apply to you.

- Be positive and honest while avoiding any negative information that may show you are not the right person for the job. And keep in mind false information can become the basis for dismissal.

- You may come across applications containing illegal and tricky questions. These may include questions about age, gender, sexual orientation, disabilities, health, marital status, children, race, arrests or convictions, religion and workers' compensation. Use N/A or a dash to answer. Additional information about illegal questions can be found at a Minnesota WorkForce Center, the state Attorney General's Office or the state Human Rights Office.

- If you have had a felony you should make the effort to meet the employer before submitting your application. This gives you a chance to sell your skills, enthusiasm and other qualities before managers learn about your offense.

- Try targeting your qualifications since many application forms have limited space to display your skills, experience and accomplishments. Display your qualifications that meet the specific needs of the job. If possible show knowledge of the employer and its products or services.

- When applying for advertised jobs or for specific positions, make sure to enter the correct job title in the blank space provided. When you aren't applying for a specific position, state the name of the department in which you wish to work. (If you have an interest in more than one advertised job, you might have to fill out more than one application.)

- If you have job gaps in your employment history, try listing positive ways you spent time while unemployed. Make your answer short, simple and truthful. Examples include managing and maintaining a household, volunteering, attending school and providing child care. If you volunteered for an organization make note of the type of work you did.

- When asked about salary requirements give a range or respond with "negotiable." Use one of these responses even if you know the wage. You never know what the future holds, and you could negotiate a higher salary. Find salary ranges at www.iseek.org, www.careeronestop.org or www.bls.gov.

You will need the month and year you started working, when you left and the reasons for your departures. Write a brief description of your duties for each position, too, because most applications include a place for that information.

Additionally, you should collect information on your degrees, certifications, honors, special training, hobbies, volunteer activities and other relevant experience that could help win you a job. For a more thorough list of what might be required, head for the Personal Data Record document at the end of this chapter.

Dealing With "Reason for Leaving"

Explaining why you left an employer can be a sensitive topic. Saying you hated your boss or the firm had a work environment akin to a prison are probably not good options. Reasons for leaving can be a tough part of the application to fill in truthfully without having your application and resume rejected by potential employers.

When responding to "reasons for leaving" choose your words carefully because negative responses may provide an easy way for the employer to eliminate you from consideration. When stating why you left a job avoid using the words "fired," "quit," "illness" or "personal reasons" because those responses may reduce your chances of being called for an interview. Always look for positive statements. You could say, for example, you returned to school to learn new skills or to find a job that more closely matched your skills.

If you were "fired" don't use that word or "terminated." Find a phrase that sounds neutral such as "involuntary separation." And then call past employers and negotiate what they will say in response to reference checks. When contacting former employers, reintroduce yourself and explain you are looking for a new job. For legal reasons chances are good they will not tell future employers you were fired, and you can ask that they simply provide your dates of employment, your job title and a description of your job duties.

Should you face termination in the future you should request that the employer's records reveal a mutually agreeable reason for separation. You don't want to hurt your future employment opportunities, and your employer may feel the same way. After all, people are asked to leave for any number of reasons that have little to do with their job abilities and more to do with a poor job match or poor fit with an organization's culture.

HOW TO ATTACH A RESUME TO AN ONLINE APPLICATION

Some online applications require you to electronically attach your resume. If you don't have a computer, buy a USB drive and save your resume to it.

Another option is opening a free account at Google Docs, which offers several online applications that mirror Microsoft's Office suite. Google has helpful videos and good explanations on its site describing how to use its Office suite and how to share content with other users.

Otherwise here's the process, and keep in mind these instructions will vary based on the application you are filling out and the software on your computer. Some job sites and employers will want you to paste your resume into an e-mail. To do this in Windows, use your cursor and highlight your entire resume, right click to "copy" the contents and then go to your e-mail. Place the cursor beneath your open e-mail message, right click and "paste" the resume into it. You can also attach your resume file to an e-mail by clicking on the attachments icon on the toolbar of an open e-mail. When you locate your resume file, click "ok" or "insert." You know your file is attached to the e-mail correctly if you can see the file name listed below the subject of your e-mail.

It's common for online applications to prompt you to attach your resume to the application itself. Usually they will provide a button on the application that links directly to your computer files. Just like attaching a resume to an e-mail, locate the correct file and click "ok" or "insert." Again, you will know the file is attached if you see the file name inserted in the application.

If you're struggling, simply go to the help button and type in "attachments" for step-by-step instructions on how to do it.

Have you quit a job? Be prepared to offer an explanation. If you left under less than favorable conditions, avoid saying anything negative about the employer and use terms such as "resigned," "wasn't a good fit" or "voluntarily separated," which imply you followed proper procedures in leaving the job. Other reasons for quitting a job include volunteer work (state what kind of work and with whom you did volunteer work), starting your own business, a scholarship or raising your family. In all of these cases, you need to assure the employer you're now fully ready to assume the responsibilities of a new job.

If you resigned for a better job, that statement better be true. That could include leaving for advancement potential, to work closer to home, to have a better work environment, higher pay or for a career change. Make certain the reason "for a better job" shows no noticeable break in employment that might raise a red flag to hiring managers who may suspect an exaggeration in the statement.

"Quitting to move to another area" for family, greater economic potential or suitability for raising children is a fine reason, but try to use it just once. If that's the reason for several job jumps you may come off as not being a dependable or stable employee. Leaving to attend school is a good enough reason, yet again make sure your application and/or resume agree. You should assure the employer any continuing school activities won't interfere with the job.

Millions of Americans have been laid off through no fault of their own. Those circumstances can be explained with phrases such as "lack of work," "lack of operating funds," "temporary employment," "seasonal employment," "company closed," "plant closing," "company downsizing" or "corporate merger." Layoffs have been such a common aspect of the employment landscape that hiring managers will not hold it against applicants since many of them — or their family members — have suffered the same fate.

In the economy of the last two decades many people have been employed in several jobs. It's no longer a shame to have a portfolio of different jobs and careers. There are employers who appreciate a reservoir of experience and understand a job market where rapid transformation and consolidation have left many workers with few options other than changing jobs.

SCREENED PROFILE:

JANET MCCULLOUGH:
THE HR PERSPECTIVE ON APPLICATIONS

Many companies want job seekers to follow a simple formula: Fill out an online application and attach a current resume.

Online or paper applications are official statements of interest in open positions, says Janet McCullough, corporate human resources manager with HickoryTech, a communications provider in Mankato, Minn.

Applications offer job seekers a way to present their qualifications along with their agreement that "all information presented in the application is honest and true statements," she says. They may contain employer requirements for drug testing, criminal background checks and other pre-employment information, McCullough says.

Take time to fill out the applications and sign them, she suggests. "First impressions are important, and even online applications have the ability to make a good or not so good first impression," says McCullough.

If the website allows you to attach a resume to your application, make sure your resume provides "not too little or too much detail." A good model is a one-page resume that captures key areas of education, experience, skills and, preferably, the three most recent employers.

"In today's market, I may receive a large number of job seekers, and I have only a short period of time to review and look for the keywords I need to see to go to the next step in the recruiting process," says McCullough.

HickoryTech's human resources staff members rarely look through the pile of resumes they have collected over several months. Instead, they look at who applied for the current opening. McCullough says: "You need to check back at our website constantly to let us know you want to apply for new openings, or you can establish an automatic e-mail to be sent to you when a position in your interest area opens up — a tool many websites use."

Gathering References, Recommendations and Other Supportive Documents

Aside from resumes and cover letters, which are discussed in Chapter 4, you should have another digital or paper folder with the following elements: recommendations, performance evaluations, references, work samples and portfolios. We explore each of those subjects in the following section.

Letters of Recommendation

Letters of recommendation are written evaluations of your work performance and work habits. Your present or previous supervisor, manager or team member usually writes them at your request. Employers have no obligation to write these recommendations and may not due to liability issues and company policy, but they may offer a reference letter if you have been a good employee.

If you are a student and have little or no work experience, you can ask your instructor, internship supervisor, adviser, mentor, coach or volunteer coordinator to write letters of recommendation. Without much work experience, especially in jobs meaningful to their careers, students will find the best method of demonstrating their skills may be through having others attest to them in letters of recommendation.

If you are new to the labor market with no paid-work experience, you can ask neighbors, volunteer coordinators, community leaders, church members or anyone else who knows you and your work ethic to write a letter of recommendation. The person recommending you needs to address how long he has known you, the quality of your work or participation, dedication, skills and work habits.

Don't be surprised if a busy reference asks you to write the first draft of the letter before she edits and signs it. It's a common practice, and feel free to oblige by highlighting in the letter your skills and achievements while working in that job or internship. The reference has the right to add or edit out anything that is not correct before signing it.

Performance Evaluation

A performance evaluation is a formal, written review or evaluation of your work. It usually covers a specific period of time and includes the quality, quantity, work habits and attitude with which you have performed your job. It can also state your promotions, demotions and reprimands. Positive performance evaluations can be included with your resume or application to bolster your credentials and increase your opportunities of securing a job.

References

Choose your references with care. Someone influential in your community or in a well-known business may be an effective reference but should not be selected for this reason alone. Look for people who honestly know you and will speak objectively. Avoid references, such as your spouse or a parent, where the potential employer may assume bias.

Avoid references that may be controversial or may concern employers. Examples of these types of references are clergy or social workers. You may even want to use different references for different employment opportunities.

Generally speaking, four types of references can be called upon for recommendations.

- *Work Related*: Includes past employers, coworkers, subordinates or clients who can speak about your specific employment experience. You can also list the people for whom you perform volunteer activities, babysitting, lawn mowing and other odd jobs.

- *Professional*: People who know you on a professional basis such as contacts from business and sales, clubs, or professional and community organizations.

- *Academic*: Instructors and vocational counselors who can speak about your academic endeavors (appropriate for current students or recent graduates).

- *Personal*: Only use a personal reference if you have no work-related, professional or academic ones to offer. Friends and neighbors who know you personally and who can describe your self-management skills are effective. Use the names of people who can tell an employer you can be depended on to do a good job.

When using people as references, get their permission first and tell them about your job search and the type of job opportunities you seek. Don't blindside them. Ask if they would be comfortable recommending you.

Find out if the reference would prefer to be contacted at work or home. Find out the best time to reach her/him so this information can be given to a prospective employer. You may need to provide the reference's occupation and phone number, how long you've known each other and the nature of the relationship.

Send your references a thank you note when you know they have given you a recommendation.

Work Samples and Portfolios

You probably heard in school the old saying "show, don't tell" or "A picture is worth a thousand words." Those sayings even make sense when considering the possibilities for showcasing your qualifications. Presenting a picture of your work accomplishments may provide immediate impact and understanding of your skills.

Today, work samples and portfolios are a major asset for most job seekers, regardless of their career field. If you have a job where you produce something, even a haircut, you can show photographic evidence of your ability. If you do not have evidence it may be time to start using your camera to capture images of your work. A chef or baker can show photographs of culinary creations.

Photographs aren't the only way to reveal your skills. Tailors or seamstresses can wear examples of the clothing they designed and sewed. An administrative assistant can offer a writing sample. A sales person might have a graph showing sales results. Staff members can present brochures, reports or newsletters as samples of their work. A mechanic can present pictures of auto restorations. Facilitators or trainers can use participant evaluations and videos of presentations. Other sources of work samples include hobbies, sports, scouts, hunting, fishing, crafts, volunteer work and other interests.

Work samples build self-confidence, prove your credibility and show your ability to finish tasks. Use them to illustrate your skills, abilities and accomplishments. After all, you're proud of what you've done and you should not feel apprehensive about showing it.

Despite the obvious advantages of having a portfolio, few employers see them during interviews. So how effective are they? Verizon Wireless "talent connector" Krystal Dominick says only three or four applicants out of the 300 interviews she conducts annually come in with a portfolio.

And how many people in that small group were hired? "All of them got jobs," she says. "The portfolios really help them showcase their experience and their job histories."

Paper Portfolios

A portfolio is a method of organizing and presenting your skills that resonate with your occupational objective. An excellent way to illustrate your skills, your career, training and education, portfolios can help display your best work and provide you with a story to tell employers about your career and the challenges you overcame in various positions.

How do you start? For a paper portfolio, begin with a loose leaf binder with dividers. The first page can be a fresh copy of your resume, or you can place that in a pocket in the front cover. The content in the rest of the portfolio is best displayed in clear page protectors.

The first section of your portfolio should be used for your research on your target company. Go to the company's website to find information about it. There you can find "about us" statements, mission or value statements, and press releases. Even include a copy of an article that shows a challenge or problem a company's industry faces. Those articles can initiate a dialogue.

In the first section you could have a page that matches your skills with those sought by an employer if you are responding to a specific job opening notice. That will address quickly why you are a serious candidate for the job since your skill set will match the position, and the fact you went to the trouble of creating a portfolio will reveal your ambition and focus.

How you organize the rest of the information in the portfolio is up to you. If your job requires working among different product categories or divisions, you can divide up the content in that way, with a handful of examples from each one. You could have partial samples of your output and offer full versions if the interviewer requests them. A 30-page PowerPoint in a portfolio is overkill, but a page or two would be fine. If the interviewer says, "I'd love to see the whole thing," e-mail it later.

As the interview moves forward, refer back to the portfolio any time you can. Look for opportunities to show and tell the employer what you have done. Each time, pull out a copy to show the interviewer. Have a photocopy available to leave behind.

The content of the portfolio will be dictated by each person's experiences. For a list of potential items to put in a portfolio, go to page 115.

CASE STUDY:
MOLLY MCGINNIS

A paralegal in search of employment in a tough legal market, Molly McGinnis created a 43-page portfolio with separate sections such as "professional profile," "honors and awards," "paralegal skills," "computer skills" and "liberal arts."

Within those sections were subsections with a resume, letters of recommendation, awards, legal writing samples and Excel and PowerPoint examples, as well as a written essay from a college course she had taken. (See McGinnis' table of contents and "mission statement" in the Endnotes section of this chapter.)

The portfolio was not easy to put together, but it has paid off. "It took me two or three months to get it all together," says McGinnis. "But having a portfolio has really helped me in interviews. It gives me more of a professional appearance. Resumes basically tell interviewers, 'I did this, I did that,' but they can't know if what you're saying is true. With a portfolio you can show what you have done and what you can do."

E-Portfolios

E-portfolios are online compilations of what was just described in the previous section. You can use many of the same components in an e-portfolio, such as work samples, photographs, personal data, resumes, references, educational backgrounds, career objectives, volunteer activities, letters of recommendation, awards, badges and military records.

Minnesota offers free to state residents the e-portfolio site www. efoliomn.com, sponsored by Minnesota State Colleges and Universities. Largely populated by students looking for jobs, the site nonetheless has attracted 90,000 registered users, many of them job seekers with lengthy careers.

After creating a site, you can e-mail a link to prospective employers, references, your network and anyone else who might have an interest. The pages are built to be clean and inviting, with a good, colorful template that allows for modification. Give it a test run to see if you can make it work for your career.

PROFILE:
JOSEPH SCHUFMAN

After 23 years with Verizon, Joseph Schufman took a generous buy-out package and signed a non-compete contract prohibiting him from working for another telecommunications company for one year.

While waiting for the year to end, Schufman, 64, created two Web-based tools — an eFolio Minnesota site and a LinkedIn.com portfolio — to tell more about his accomplished career.

"It took four hours for me to create an eFolio site, and that became my website," says Schufman "By having it on LinkedIn.com I could tell many people who viewed my profile also went to my website. It's a great tool."

One of those potential employers who viewed both sites was ISoft, an information technology outsourcer, which hired Schufman for a sales executive position. "I'm glad I spent the time to create a portfolio. It showcased my career and my abilities perhaps better than a traditional resume."

Personal Websites

Another option is to use online Web creation sites — there are several — that allow you to create a limited number of pages for free. You will pay for more pages through a monthly subscription. The free site, however, may be just enough to get your Web presence going.

What's good about websites and e-portfolios is that employers can see what you have done in a visual presentation that is not available in a written resume. If they like what they see on the resume and want to learn more about you, they can quickly skim your e-portfolio or website. The fact you developed an online presence will be impressive enough, and the work exhibited there should only help your cause. As in the past, make sure everything is spelled correctly, reads well and links to content work.

When you get to the interview, you can have the individual pull up the digital portfolio to assist in the discussion. With a paper or e-portfolio and/or a job website, you will have a nice assortment of informational sources describing your skills, career, values and volunteer pursuits. Having the website and e-portfolio will only strengthen your online presence in a positive way, a clear advantage when a potential employer decides to Google your name.

POTENTIAL PORTFOLIO CONTENT DIVISIONS

- Employer/Industry Information (articles on the interviewer, employer and industry)
- Personal Information
- Project and Work Samples
- Skills List, Matched to Job
- Diplomas, Certifications, Transcripts, Special Licenses
- Workshops and Conferences
- References, Evaluations, Letters of Recommendation and Testimonials
- Awards
- Letters of Thanks
- Articles About You
- Stories Demonstrating Skills or Character (preferably signed)
- Writing Samples/Published Work
- Documentation/Photos of Speaking Events
- Presentations (computer, hard copy, etc.)
- Teamwork Examples
- "Before" and "After" Examples
- Leadership Examples
- Work Showing Computer Savvy, Such as Charts, Spreadsheets, Graphics, etc.
- Job Match Letter
- Questions for the Employer
- Note Pad

ENDNOTES

PERSONAL DATA RECORD

Name	
Address	
Social Security Number	
Phone Numbers	Home Fax
E-mail	
Any Felony Convictions?	YES ☐ NO ☐ If yes, explain:
Employment Desired	
Position Title	Starting Wage
Dates Available	
Available for Work (circle)	Full Time Weekend Part Time On Call Temporary Seasonal Rotating Shifts

EDUCATION

	High School	Business, Trade School, College	Undergraduate	College/ University	Graduate/ Professional	Military Training
School Name/GED						
School Location						
Years Completed	Don't complete this information for high school— it either doesn't apply or could lead to age discrimination.					
Diploma/Degree						
Graduation Date						
Course of Study						
Describe Any Scholastic Honors, Assistantships, Etc.						
Describe Any Specialized Training, Assistantships, Etc.						
Foreign Languages						
Occupational License, Certifications, Registrations, Professional Affiliations						

PERSONAL DATA RECORD (continued)

EMPLOYMENT HISTORY
(list most recent employment first)

Employer Name/Organization	Address			
Dates Employed— From: Month/Year			To: Month/Year	
Job Title/Major Responsibilities/Skills, Knowledge and Abilities				
Supervisor/ Leader	Contact? Yes No		Phone	
Reason for Leaving		Ending Salary		

Employer Name/Organization	Address			
Dates Employed— From: Month/Year			To: Month/Year	
Job Title/Major Responsibilities/Skills, Knowledge and Abilities				
Supervisor/ Leader	Contact? Yes No		Phone	
Reason for Leaving		Ending Salary		

Employer Name/Organization	Address			
Dates Employed— From: Month/Year			To: Month/Year	
Job Title/Major Responsibilities/Skills, Knowledge and Abilities				
Supervisor/ Leader	Contact? Yes No		Phone	
Reason for Leaving		Ending Salary		

VOLUNTEER ACTIVITY

Dates Volunteered— From: Month/Year			To: Month/Year	
Title/Major Responsibilities/Skills, Knowledge and Abilities				
Supervisor/ Leader	Contact? Yes No		Phone	
Other Skills, Knowledge and Abilities Not Listed Above Acquired Through Hobbies or Interests				

MOLLY MCGINNIS' MISSION STATEMENT
AND PORTFOLIO TABLE OF CONTENTS

Mission Statement

*To become a team member of success in a rewarding
paralegal position with a quality law firm.*

*To utilize my experience, interest and skills in a dynamic law firm
that offers challenges and professional development.*

Table of Contents

NOTES

CHAPTER 6

How People Find Work

"Find a job you like and you add five days to every week."

— H. JACKSON BROWN JR., AUTHOR OF "LIFE'S LITTLE INSTRUCTION BOOK"

Today, companies are more selective in hiring employees due to a number of factors. They range from an overwhelming number of candidates to the economic climate, from employment legislation to new technologies, and from employer liability to organizational restructuring.

The average American will have many jobs and change careers many times during his or her lifetime. For some people — not all — a 21st century lesson of life is this: Get used to searching for a job. You are unlikely to stay at one employer, or even one career, your entire working life.

Employers seek job applicants by using a variety of approaches. We're going to take you through the most common methods. A later chapter will speak to the evolving world of social media and how some innovative employers are using platforms such as LinkedIn and Facebook to find workers.

How Employers Operate

Understanding how employers hire — and where to find open positions in today's market — will help you tremendously in landing a job. You will need to consider and act upon ideas for impressing employers with your skills, background and knowledge. Knowing how employers think and presenting yourself effectively to them is the key to success.

But it isn't easy. And the bottom line is that while you may "get" how employers hire new people, there will be times when you will be baffled, upset and mystified by the processes and outcomes.

Some employers may contact you with great interest and then not return your phone calls. You might get an interview and be assured of a position only to find the company had to pull back due to an acquisition, or the economy, or half a dozen other reasons that make sense or don't make sense.

On the good days you will discover a host of decent employers who like what you have to offer and sincerely want to speak to you. Ideally, you should roll with the punches. Prepare for potential setbacks but maintain a sense of optimism. The way you will feel when you get that new job will outweigh any setbacks incurred along the way.

The Hiring Process

Larger employers have a formal hiring structure and often involve several people in the process. In contrast, smaller employers may have one individual assigned to handling the hiring, and the process may be less formal. Other issues arise. Industry-specific practices found in medicine, education and government have unique hiring stages perhaps influenced by union contracts.

Not everyone in the structure has the authority to add new employees. Typically, a manager of the department where the person will work makes the final decision. When possible find out who makes the final decision. However, treat everyone as though they are the hiring authority during your encounters with potential employers. Kindness and curiosity can go a long way toward impressing employers and their staffs during the interviewing processes.

You will hear a lot about human resources departments. They manage the process, sometimes taking a first swipe at a pile of resumes and reducing their numbers by removing unqualified or under-qualified applicants. HR may be assigned to appointing entry-level applicants to positions, but the majority of its work involves recruiting, screening and scheduling interviews. Don't underestimate its influence when you're dealing with an employer.

Hiring practices vary based on particular industries, employers and hiring managers. Generally, however, employers follow a few common hiring strategies and tools to select candidates. It comes down to three stages: recruitment, screening and selection.

Stage 1: Recruitment

Employers need an applicant pool to fill job openings. Employers who do extensive hiring may continuously recruit applicants even when they have no immediate need. The reason? To always have a deep pool of applicants. Employers who hire occasionally, or for very specialized positions, often recruit as needed. Others may be planning a future expansion and want to know if they could fill their labor needs. Actively recruiting does not always mean actual job openings.

Companies get the word out on jobs in a variety of ways, ranging from word of mouth, to advertising (on company websites, and in online and offline newspapers and trade publications), to hiring personnel staffing services to asking employees to refer qualified candidates to them.

Stage 2: Screening

Once employers have an applicant pool, they narrow it down to the best qualified candidates. This comes after dozens, or hundreds, of applicants have been screened out of the pool. During the initial screening, employers usually spend no more than a few seconds on each application.

Larger companies often use applicant tracking systems to efficiently screen large applicant pools. Applicant tracking systems are designed to select candidates who have the desired qualifications for the job. The resume section in Chapter 4 addresses the need to consider those tracking systems when putting together your resume.

Stage 3: Selection

Interviews are the key part of the hiring process. Companies use interviews to verify qualifications and to evaluate how you will fit into the organization. If you get a call for an interview, that means you passed one hurdle and are in the running for a position. It will be up to you to convince a company that you are the best qualified person for the job.

"Best qualified" can mean many things: skills, experience, education, motivation, a passion for excellence, and a dedication to continuous learning and quality. Companies want value for their money because every employee is a major expense in terms of salary and benefits. You have to convince an employer you are the best qualified.

Where to Find Jobs

Finding job openings can seem fairly easy. Head for a huge job site like Monster.com, and it looks as though half the companies in the United States have openings. When you submit an application or resume you will find in many cases the competition numbers hundreds of people who also are using popular job websites. Still, an argument can be made that keeping an eye on those sites is not a bad idea since they will indicate which fields are growing and what companies are hiring.

Let's look at the most common sources of jobs and their pluses and minuses for job seekers.

Advertised Jobs

Job openings can be found in trade journals, job boards, company websites, social networking services, newspapers, grocery stores, libraries and store windows. The most common of these are Internet job boards.

There are drawbacks to seeking advertised jobs. They often result in competition with hundreds of applicants. Not all jobs are advertised as companies move to posting jobs on their own websites and not on large job boards. Paul Sears, an employment counselor at the Minneapolis WorkForce Center, says he firmly believes WorkForce Center customers who crowd the computer terminals in his building's lobby "should spend more time on other job-hunting activities. I wish I could tell them to stop surfing the Web for jobs and start talking to people and networking. That's how you find a job."

Still, advertised jobs should not be overlooked. Here's a strategy for spending just enough but not too much time on positions listed in publications or on the Internet.

- Pick your sources for advertised jobs — specific Internet job boards, trade journals or newspapers. Review new listings when they're released.

- Don't waste time scanning several Internet job boards. Focus your efforts on one general job board and two or three niche sites specific to your industry or field.

- Respond to new openings immediately and don't bother responding to listings that run continuously or are old.

- Take caution when responding to blind ads, which require you to apply to an anonymous e-mail address or P.O. Box. Do not apply to any jobs that don't appear to be from legitimate sources and never give out confidential information like Social Security or credit card numbers. And avoid "work from home" offers.

- Look at all the jobs listed, not just those that fit your goal, because you may find an employer you want to pursue. If they have an opening in one field, they may have one in your area of expertise, too, that isn't advertised.

- Follow up your application with a phone call to the employer.

Networking

Employment experts agree that most job openings are never advertised. Only by knocking do doors open. Creative job searching demands a lot of calling, handshaking, chatting, explaining and conversing. Improving on your networking skills can help get you through the door to employers. The hidden job market, defined as positions that go unadvertised, cannot really be pursued by you without a strong effort at networking.

A formal networking campaign is a good idea, but try not to make the folks you meet feel as though you're using them in any way. Start by speaking to people you know well, such as friends, family, neighbors and former (or current) coworkers. These people have the most interest in your success and are excellent networking contacts. Now, contact people who pop up only occasionally in your life and career. More than 25 percent of the people who find jobs through networking received the referral from someone they see once a year or less. Ask this group for ideas and referrals, remind them of who you are and ask if they might be willing to meet for a 15-minute chat. Remember, honor that time limitation unless they insist on having you stay longer (a likely scenario since most people don't time conversations).

Next, join job seeking networking groups in your industry, city or church. Minnesota WorkForce Centers sponsor a host of networking groups around the state. You may get a tip or two from other participants in the group, along with solace, advice, conversation and camaraderie.

Take those referrals and begin contacting them. These are the individuals you do not know, so you need to call and formally introduce yourself while highlighting the people who gave you their names. It's not an easy task and not everyone will call back or agree to meet. Still, these are the people who may have the responsibility for hiring or know the appropriate individual in their companies for you to contact.

Finally, we suggest cold-calling. This is picking out companies where you would like to work and cold-calling managers or employees, asking them for informational interviews or ideas for finding a job where they work. They may avoid returning your call or tell you they have little to offer in the way of open positions. Still like that company? Try another division, or move down the list to the next prospective company in your sights.

It's a good idea to look at our "Networking Log" at the end of this chapter or develop your own template. Write down the people you contacted, their phone numbers and any leads they offered. If someone doesn't return your inquiry after a couple of calls, move on. Don't be a pest because that reputation could come back to haunt you.

Take notes during interviews, and afterward write an e-mail and a personal handwritten thank you to people who took the time to speak to you. Do not overstay your welcome, and focus on getting the information you require in an informational interview. Always ask for more contacts, too, to broaden your list.

Networking is not begging. The idea is not to ask for jobs but to ask for information that may lead to a job. Usually your networking contacts will not be potential employers. They will be people who know about potential jobs or individuals in an industry who can help. If you discover contacts are potential employers with job openings that fit your skills, change gears and begin to sell yourself.

Job Fairs

Many different organizations have job fairs featuring employers willing to speak to potential employees. Ideally, job seekers have a chance to actually meet company representatives who can help them find employment.

It's a great networking opportunity because job seekers have a chance to speak directly to employers. And in a perfect world, those employers have jobs to offer.

Job fairs can be a mixed experience. Attend them with the hope of making a few connections. You may find them worth your time or you may find your efforts are better spent pursuing other avenues of employment.

TIPS FOR SUCCESSFUL NETWORKING CONVERSATIONS

- Keep the conversation focused.

- Relax. Networking conversations have specific goals, but that doesn't mean they can't be fun.

- Be curious and take an interest in the person you are networking with first.

- Be a journalist and ask lots of pertinent questions.

- Ask for help after having developed rapport. Speak of your career goals and ask if they have any advice, resources or tips to help you.

- Work hard to remember names, just like great politicians. When the person introduces herself, repeat her name back to her, as in: "It's a pleasure to meet you, Maria. My name is Joe."

- Ask for contact information. You'll need this to follow up.

- Keep your promises. If you offered to help someone else in a job search, always make good on your promises.

- Always follow up when you make a connection with a thank you note.

Making Contact With Employers

The goal of any job search campaign is to meet face-to-face with employers in an interview. The more interviews you have, the greater your chances for success. Most job seekers, however, prefer a passive job search strategy in which they submit an application or resume and wait. When they don't hear anything they start all over again by answering another ad or contacting a company only through e-mail or regular mail.

Instead of those passive attempts at getting a job, try a more active approach by taking initiative and making direct contact with potential employers.

Direct employer contact requires preparation, confidence and persistence. Many people are uncomfortable with this tactic, afraid of offending the employers with too much aggressiveness. Yet going straight to an employer works, even if you already answered an advertised job. Showing a strong desire to work for a company without becoming too bothersome — a fine line to tread — will likely yield success faster than answering online ads.

PROFILE:

KARLA BONINE'S WARM CONTACTS

As a human resource professional for more than 17 years, Karla Bonine had studied thousands of resumes and worked on hiring hundreds of people.

Having seen every conceivable strategy for getting a job, Bonine felt nearly paralyzed when the proverbial shoe was on the other foot. She was now the one looking for a job after losing hers. Bonine found networking and finding a new position to be a tad uncomfortable.

"I discovered I don't do cold-calling well. I prefer what I call 'warm contacts.' That's a person who knows someone I know well," she says.

Thinking of the job hunt as a chance to practice her "networking skills," she made a minimum of five personal contacts a week.

Forty contacts and coffee klatches later a former client of hers called with news of an open position. She got the job and is now a senior benefits analyst.

"I remember when people cold-called me, and I tried to remember what worked best when I had to do my own cold-calling," she says. "I would say when calling someone attitude is everything."

Richard Bolles, the celebrated author of "What Color is Your Parachute?", says networking is by far the most effective way to get a job. He cites research that looked at the different methods of finding an opening, such as answering ads or using private employment agencies. It revealed that job hunters who make direct contact with potential employers were astonishingly successful.

- 86 percent of people found jobs after conducting a skills inventory and identifying new environments and careers. That is 12 times more effective than sending out resumes.

- 84 percent of individuals found jobs when, as part of a job club, they leafed through the Yellow Pages to find subjects and fields of interest. Then, these individuals called companies and asked if they had any openings.

- 69 percent found jobs using this same method, only doing it solo and not as part of a job club. Being part of a job club seems to help, but even doing it alone works. "For perspective, however, note that by doing targeted phone calls by yourself, you have an almost 10 times better chance of finding a job, than if you sent out your resume," Bolles wrote.

- 47 percent who found jobs personally went to companies in their communities and inquired about employment without any prior knowledge of job openings.

- 33 percent used job leads from their networks to land employment.

LOOKING IN YOUR BACKYARD

Having been let go by a major hotel chain due to a decline in business, Lisa Stallman figured her next job would likely be in something other than the hit-hard-by-the-recession hospitality industry.

In looking for a new job, Stallman, a two-decade veteran of hotel management, had the goal of staying close to home in the vicinity of Brooklyn Park, Minn., and the northwest Twin Cities suburbs in order to be close to her children and husband.

One day while traveling down Wyoming Avenue and 93rd Street she pulled over into a parking lot of an office park, took out of her wallet a store receipt and began writing on the back of it the names of businesses at that location.

Then, Stallman went home and began to research those companies to see if they had openings. She looked into firms in fitness, book publishing and convention exhibits before calling Coffee Mill Inc., a company providing hot and cold beverages to offices in the Twin Cities region.

The owner of the family-operated business spoke to Stallman several times before hiring her within a span of just two weeks. As a "sales associate," Stallman has a chance to use her hospitality training and connections to win clients.

The search may have been unconventional, but it worked. "It was a matter of going out and meeting my neighbors — both businesses and people in our neighborhood — and letting them know I was looking for a job," she says. "It's great to be able to find one good opportunity not far from my front door."

Basic Principles of Direct Employer Contact

Networking and research will land you plenty of names of companies and individuals within them as contacts while pursuing a job.

Are you ready to contact employers directly? Good, because it works. Now, let's look at effective ways to do it.

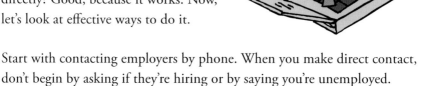

Start with contacting employers by phone. When you make direct contact, don't begin by asking if they're hiring or by saying you're unemployed.

Avoid being transferred to the human resources department unless you have been told it is the hiring authority. If you hear you should submit an application or resume, ask if you can have an informational interview either by phone or in person. Tell the individuals with whom you speak that you're less interested in simply sending in a resume and more interested in learning about the company. Should you receive a brush off and request to send the resume, kindly say you will abide by the company's process and that you will stay in touch following your submission of job-related materials.

Whenever possible, make the next step your responsibility — not the employer's. For example, if an employer says, "We will call you in a couple of weeks," you could respond with, "Would it be all right if I call you two weeks from today?" If they say, "Yes," then you've agreed on your follow-up, and the responsibility is yours.

When you contact an employer, you might reach a receptionist before speaking with a manager or executive. Think of receptionists and other "gatekeepers" as the eyes and ears of decision makers. Receptionists tend to put in a good word for people who treat them with courtesy and respect.

Should you get an informational interview, conduct research on the company prior to your appointment. We have plenty of details on researching companies elsewhere in this book, and we suggest you take a look at it. And expect rejection. It goes with the territory. Don't take it personally. Maintain a good attitude and a healthy sense of humor.

PROFILE:

CORRINE CASANOVA CITES IMPORTANCE OF PHONING

Health care writer Corrine Casanova spent several months looking for writing and editing jobs on the Web and e-mailing former colleagues to chat and ask for any employment leads.

It was a comfortable strategy, but few job or freelance leads trickled in. After attending a Creative Job Search class, she decided to start calling potential employers outside her network.

A suburban Minneapolis hospital marketing staffer told Casanova the inquiry came at the right time and that some freelance assignments could be on the way. Another call to a former competitor brought news of a position in Nevada that might become available soon.

"I thought I was pretty connected, but it wasn't helpful using e-mail and the Web almost exclusively," says Casanova. "In picking up the phone and calling people that I did not know, I opened the door to freelancing opportunities and potential full-time opportunities."

Telephoning Tips

Although the Internet is quickly becoming the most popular mode of communication, the telephone remains a critical tool in a successful job search campaign. The Internet may be a great way to research jobs and companies, but the telephone is the best way to make direct employer contact and to open the doors of opportunity.

Effective telephone techniques are critical skills all job seekers need, and they can be learned. You need to learn how to script a call, the basics of sounding competent on a phone and the importance of having a follow-up strategy that appeals to employers.

Some people have a hard time with the idea of selling their qualifications over the phone. Nobody wants to sound pushy or unprepared, but learning how to sell yourself is critical to a successful job search.

Just like a sales call, you will get about 20 seconds to capture the employer's attention. Therefore, communication has to be to the point and concise. Even the best communicators use scripting to make sure they get their point across. It helps to relieve jitters and keep the conversation focused.

Have an objective for the call. You may be seeking information, trying to schedule a meeting or presenting your qualifications to a potential employer. Have a secondary objective. Often you won't achieve your primary objective, but every telephone call is an opportunity to seek information.

A MODEL TELEPHONE SCRIPT

Caller: Hi. This is Jerry Job. I'm trying to contact the person in charge of marketing. Who would that be?

Receiver: That's Lisa Ramirez. She is the director.

Caller: I would like to contact her. Does she have a direct number or an extension number?

Receiver: Her direct number is 555-5555. Would you like me to transfer you?

Caller: Please do.

A MODEL FOLLOW-UP SCRIPT

Caller: Hello. This is Jerry Job. I interviewed for the computer programmer position last week. I'm just checking to see if the hiring decision has been made.

Receiver: Not yet. We anticipate making our final selection this Wednesday.

Caller: I'm still very interested in the position. You're doing some very innovative multimedia work that's cutting edge. You have a bright and energetic technical staff and working with them really appeals to me. Would it be OK if I called you on Wednesday? What's a good time?

Make a call to get the name of the person you want to speak to and then either have the operator transfer you or redial and make a direct call to that individual.

Outline in writing what you want to say. This is important in the early stages of cold-calling or when the call is important. Later on, you'll script most of your calls in your head. Don't read your script. Your presentation should be natural.

The script will depend on the goal of the call and whether you know the person you are calling. A good script should include an introduction that describes who you are and whether you were referred. State the purpose of your call and then ask for information or to schedule the meeting.

PHONE SKILLS 101

- Practice your skills on a spouse or friend. Tape yourself to hear how you sound.

- Deal with voice mail. Leave your name and phone number (twice, and slowly) and the reason for the call. Be upbeat, simple, clear and concise. Avoid the monotone. If you are offered the option to review your message, do so just to check it.

- If you have an answering machine, make sure your message is polite and professional. It's not cute or clever, by the way, to have your children do the message on a phone line that will be used by potential employers.

- Organize all your job search materials nearby and take notes.

- Listen carefully. If you sense you've called at a bad time, politely ask if there's a better time. Listen for "buy" signals, among them questions about qualifications or about other topics. They're showing an interest in you.

- Handle objections such as "We're looking for someone with more experience or education" or "Sorry, we're not hiring right now" with a response that continues to sell your qualifications.

- Follow up: The persistent 20 percent make 80 percent of the sales. While you have the contact on the telephone, agree on when you'll call back. Keep a follow-up calendar and maintain a record of your contacts. If someone agrees to call you, give a time you can be reached — or your mobile phone number.

- Stand up during cold calls. Being erect will improve your posture and expand your lungs, making you sound more alert.

- If you can't get past the receptionist, try before 8 a.m., during lunch, after 5 p.m. or Saturday morning. If you still can't get through, solicit the receptionist's assistance.

- Look for ways to compliment the person or the company. Sell your strengths, skills and accomplishments.

E-mailing Tips

E-mail is the easiest way to apply for a
job opening and the easiest inquiry for
employers to avoid. If you catch a manager
on the phone you can try to make a quick
pitch. You may hear a grunt and a "Sorry,
we're not hiring" or a "Hey, why don't you
come in. Let's set up a time." Managers are
usually overwhelmed with internal and external
e-mails daily, so trying to capture their attention can be difficult.

A more creative strategy combines e-mail, calling and mailing managers your
information. Call it the one-two digital/verbal punch.

The approach is to e-mail the prospect a short letter of just a paragraph saying
you're interested in an advertised job or you're wondering if any positions
are currently open. Stress that you will call within a day or two. Skip writing
a long cover letter — unless an advertised job has been posted — because
effective e-mails tend to be brief. In a case of an available opening, many
employers recommend making the e-mail message the cover letter.

Attach your resume, written in Word or as an Adobe PDF document, to
e-mail correspondence related to finding a job. Managers can open either
format with little problem. Then call within a day or two and, if leaving a
message, remind the individual of the day and time you sent the e-mail and
attachment and spell your name. E-mail programs can segment messages by
day, time, subject line and sender. The person can locate it faster with the
information you just provided.

Then print out and send via U.S. mail what you e-mailed. This illustrates your
high level of interest in the position and the company, and your commitment
to making certain the manager and others at the firm see your resume.

Counseling and Personnel Staffing Services

Personnel staffing services and contract firms can be excellent job search resources. Organized as private or nonprofit public entities, they specialize in service to specific groups of companies and employment clients. For example, a common field such as information technology will be the focus of dozens of contract firms in a large metropolitan area. A smaller number of staffing firms may work specifically to assist people with disabilities in finding jobs.

Each firm is unique and may provide a combination of blended services. The type of services offered may be influenced by whom they represent: you or the employer. Generally, their focus is on matching your skills with the job openings of employers or companies. Depending on your circumstances and needs, these outsourcing companies benefit you in securing employment. They fall into several categories.

Staffing/Recruiting: Employers use staffing services to assist them in filling their job openings. Staffing agencies recruit, perform extensive interviewing, check references and submit only the most qualified applicants to the employer. Some staffing services offer a bulletin board service where job orders and/or resumes are posted and job seekers and employers interact without any agency interference.

Job Search Training: Minnesota WorkForce Centers and other workforce centers around the country, as well as staffing services, offer specific training in job search skills to enable you to successfully find your own job. This training may include individual workshops and materials on a variety of job search topics. Classes, which usually are free, focus on resume writing, interviewing and so forth. If offered by private companies a fee will be charged.

Career Counseling and Planning: If you're looking for a job or entering the labor market for the first time, consider talking with a career counselor to help you with self-assessment, knowledge of the labor market, employment trends and training opportunities. These companies offer aptitude, interest, personality and skills testing to help you with career changes and to fulfill your potential by matching you to employment opportunities.

Outplacement or Career Transition: When companies downsize their workforces, some firms provide laid-off employees with outplacement assistance such as job search workshops and materials, phone rooms, job leads, resume design, a job club and employment counseling. Ask your employer if these services will be provided.

Temporary and Contract Employment: These firms refer you to temporary employment opportunities as requested by an employer who specifies the job requirements and time period of the work assignment. You work for the temporary or contract firm during this time and they pay you. By performing well you may get a full-time offer after your contract ends. Some positions, however, fill only short-term or seasonal needs, such as during the holiday rush or in summer.

Benefits of Being a Contract Worker

Of the personnel service arrangements available, being a contract or temporary employee is the most advantageous. By working in contract jobs you can build skills and meet financial needs while continuing to look for permanent work. It's easier to get a job when you have a job. You might get more flexible hours or working conditions to accommodate your personal situation as well as help with transportation, testing, training, child care and health care.

This type of employment can also be useful for those who need to gain work experience, develop skills, get training or increase networking contacts. It's also a good way to check out an employer or an occupation before making a

TEMPORARY JOBS

commitment to training, a career path or a particular employer. Personnel staffing services offer a variety of services and options for the job seeker, but keep in mind the following considerations when looking for temporary employment:

- Check into the temp firm's reputation. Determine if any fees will be charged for services before accepting or signing anything.

- Staffing services work with the job market daily and can provide valuable information that's helpful in your job search. Treat them as you'd treat a potential employer because they can expose you to many opportunities that are otherwise not available.

- If you're working with a staffing service, don't assume you can sit back and wait for jobs. Continue your search.

- Temporary staffing services are your employers when you're on assignment for them. Ask about items you need to know before you agree to accept employment. You need to know the pay rate, benefits, estimated length of assignment, the chance of becoming an employee of the company and what's expected of you. Also, let them know the hours and days you're available, your overtime availability, and your transportation and salary needs.

- Consider the secondary objectives of the service. An example might be career counseling provided by training or educational institutions. They may have a primary interest in enrolling you in their training program for funding reasons.

- Check out their placement rates and services with the Department of Education, Better Business Bureau or with former students.

- If you're receiving unemployment insurance benefits, you should realize short-term wages may affect eligibility and benefit amounts.

The Worst Ways to Find a Job

"What Color is Your Parachute?" author Richard Bolles, a longtime observer of the job market, believes the following strategies will not help you get a job. He suggests that a combination of these relatively ineffective approaches with others, especially networking, should result in a better chance of landing employment.

- Seven percent of people who only mail resumes as their strategy for finding work actually get a job.

- Seven percent who only answer ads in their field find jobs.

- Five to 24 percent who only answer ads in newspapers find jobs, a figure surely dropping alongside newspaper circulation.

- Five to 28 percent scored work by using private employment agencies or search firms.

Networking with a purpose and cold-calling companies where you want to work are the most effective means of finding employment, he suggests. Those present the most challenging methods of finding jobs, yet the alternative of answering online ads and responding to job boards will likely be equally frustrating.

Unfortunately, no easy path exists to finding a job. You will have to cold-call companies or show up at their offices and ask about employment. You'll have to network in professional groups, at your church, at your local WorkForce Center. You'll have to answer ads. You'll have to do it all, unless you find an opening early in your search.

ENDNOTES

NETWORKING LOG

It's important to document and follow up on all job leads. Use this sheet for keeping track of all your networking activity. Always ask your contacts to suggest other contacts. Keep at it.

Employer Name:	
Contact Name:	
Address :	
Fax :	
E-mail Address:	
Action Plan:	
Appointment Date/ Time:	
Follow up:	
Summary of Conversation/ Contact :	
Additional Contacts Received	

CHAPTER 7

Using the Internet and Social Media

"You're doing a great disservice to yourself by not having that kind of presence online."

— KATHLEEN TAYLOR, AUTHOR OF "HOW TO SUCCEED IN BUSINESS USING LINKEDIN: MAKING CONNECTIONS AND CAPTURING OPPORTUNITIES ON THE WORLD'S #1 BUSINESS NETWORKING SITE"

The Internet has been a boon and a bane for job seekers. It offers a repository of listed jobs around the corner and around the world. You can find an opening in your field in five minutes. And you can discover just as quickly that 500 people have applied for that same particular opening.

Many job counselors warn that the Internet can be a giant swamp where you can apply and apply and apply — day after day after day — to no avail. As author Richard Bolles has pointed out, just 4 to 7 percent of people ever find a job using only the Internet. Should you even bother using the Internet to search?

The answer: absolutely. It is wise to spend a few minutes a day tracking openings in your field and your area, but not a few hours. Many companies have begun listing their job openings primarily on their corporate websites, a practice that saves them money and keeps the job pool, to a degree, filled by people interested in working there. An advertisement on a company's "job openings" section and not on job boards will appeal to people checking that company's website. However, some aggregators simply pull those openings off corporate America's websites, opening them to a broader audience.

In dealing with the Internet, focus is important. In its hyperlinked universe, it remains too easy for users to link off to site after site, avoiding the goal of finding a job by learning about random, unrelated subjects. Stay the course; if you lose track, log off. To keep you going we've created a game plan of simple tools you can employ to keep your browsing to a minimum and your networking and information gathering to a maximum.

Cheat Sheet for Digital Job Hunting

Internet browsers such as Explorer and Firefox are remarkably sophisticated today. If you have visited a website a few times the browser will automatically pull it up in the future after just a few keystrokes. You can create bookmarks — called "favorites" in Explorer and "bookmarks" in Firefox — of sites you visit frequently and divide them so you can access them more easily. Here's some advice on the tools you should use to make the most of your Internet searches.

<u>*Search engines*</u>: The fundamental tool for finding information on the Internet is the search engine. Search engines use keywords to help you find what you are looking for on the Internet. The list generated from your search can then be used to track down jobs and learn more about companies you are targeting. Mastering these tools is critical to effectively and efficiently locating information on the Internet. Google.com and bing.com are two examples of popular search engines.

<u>*Websites*</u>: Organizations and businesses publish websites that provide information about their businesses online. The quality and amount of information that is provided varies among sites. Visiting a company's website is the first place to go when researching specific employers. You may often find vision and mission statements, a history of the organization, names of key employers and supervisors, business plans and job postings.

Employment sites: These sites, sometimes called "job boards," are the most popular way to find job leads on the Internet. Similar to search engines, users can put keywords into a search bar to find jobs based on their personal criteria. They help you get more specific results by location, field, industry or job title. One of the most common mistakes that job seekers make is spending too many hours browsing job boards for openings. Keep it to a minimum; your chances of finding a position listed on a job board are slim.

Job expert Peter Weddles came up with a strategy for using job boards that goes like this: 1GJ = 2GB + 3 NB. Translation: 1 Good Job = 2 General Boards + 3 Niche Boards. General job boards list thousands of jobs from thousands of employers, the drawback being the popularity of these sites can be a disadvantage. For this reason, dedicate more of your attention to niche job boards focusing on openings in specific industries.

Online periodicals: The Internet is the fastest way to access published information. Newspapers, magazines and trade

---

CASE STUDY:

A MINNESOTAN FINDS WORK THE NEW FASHION WAY

Rachel Pinneg is member of a new generation of job seekers who communicate with friends and learn of open positions through social networks.

While a graduate student in library science at the University of St. Catherine in St. Paul, Pinneg began using PB Works, a collaboration platform. She liked it so much she asked the Silicon Valley company if it had any needs for a part-time employee, one who happened to live in St. Paul.

The company liked her resume and agreed to work out an arrangement. Then Pinneg's husband, Matt, got a job at Apple. The couple moved to the Bay Area and PB Works asked Pinneg to work full time.

Eventually, she managed 12 people at PB Works, but she was restless. Pinneg set up a few RSS feeds, which are automated services that alert subscribers when their favorite sites have been updated. After setting an RSS feed on Craigslist, she learned of another job at a startup called Syncplicity.

Now, she's at Syncplicity. "Everyone pretty much uses social media out here," says Pinneg, 26. "It's all very networking based, whether it's through Facebook, or Twitter, or networking events. Social media is just another way to network."

---

journals can all be found online. Trade journals contain articles by industry experts, information about networking events, suggestions on industry blogs and jobs. To find a trade journal related to your search, try typing "trade journal directory" into a search engine. Or, go to your public library for help accessing trade journal and professional association databases.

Association websites: Almost every industry has an association with a website full of information on trends, volunteer or professional development opportunities, best practices, industry news and, inevitably, a job board. It may require membership in the organization to get at the really good content and the job board, and you'll have to determine whether the fee is worth it. Most charge annual fees, but if you can buy a six-month membership you'll then have the time to check the site and determine whether it yields content that helps you find employment.

Tips for Internet Job Searches

Using the Internet for research isn't the same as surfing the Internet. Researching is centered, surfing is wandering. Stay focused on your research goal. If you find something interesting en route to your goal, bookmark the site and come back to it. Here is some guidance on not getting lost in the murk of the Web.

Develop a research strategy: Develop a plan before you begin looking for information. Decide in advance how much time you're willing to invest. Your topic will influence where you look. Knowing roughly where your information might be found will help in developing your plan. Remember, "Plan your work, then work your plan."

Keep records: It's important to keep a record of your research. As you explore potential employers, industries and communities, you will collect a lot of information. Discard that which has little or no immediate value, then file and maintain information that you want to keep. Almost every Internet newbie has given in to the temptation to bookmark sites without discretion. The result is almost always an unmanageable tangle of Internet bookmarks.

Set goals: Stay on track and have a goal. "I'm going to spend the next hour researching two potential employers who might need someone with marketing skills" is far better stated than "I'm going to look for jobs on the Internet."

Posting Your Resume to Internet Sites

Many employers manage and sort resumes in a resume database. They search the database for specific skills and qualifications, so a well-written resume with the right skills and qualifications will show up frequently and prominently in the employer's search. One advantage to you is that your resume will usually stay current in the database much longer than in a filing cabinet. If the resume doesn't show up in a search today, it has a chance of showing up in a search in the future.

There are several common ways that a resume is placed into a database. It may be entered directly to a job board or at an employer's website or scanned from paper. Any resume (paper or electronic) may find its way into a database. Many sites allow you to update in standard formats such as Word or as a PDF. Pay attention to the directions on the website for uploading resumes and cover letters; a good first impression for a potential employee is the ability to follow directions.

Newsgroups are another place where you can post your resume. Most newsgroups are discussion forums where people who share similar interests can exchange and browse messages. Professional newsgroups are excellent

places to meet people, but they often ask people not to post resumes. It's considered a bad habit. If you make a job contact through a professional online newsgroup you can always follow up with a private e-mail and resume.

Some newsgroups do, in fact, list job openings or post resumes. Many progressive recruiters look in these newsgroups for qualified candidates, and it may be worth your effort to have your resume posted on these sites. Again, pay attention. You might be limited to uploading your resume as a text file.

Keep a few things in mind about posting resumes to newsgroups. Many resume databases also have a specific period during which individuals can keep their resumes active. You will have to reactivate your resume after the time lapses or, if you get a job, you should take the time to remove it.

Resume posting to newsgroups might open you up to spam, so you may want to use a separate online account, such as Google Gmail, Yahoo or Hotmail, to deal with mail generated from newsgroups. Be prepared to screen out the advertisements. Remember, if it sounds too good to be true, it probably is.

If you're contacted from a posting, screen people carefully before you give any additional information or schedule a meeting. Ask for a phone number where you can call them back and search their name online to determine if they have a website, participate in online activities and have contributed comments to online groups.

Don't be offended if recruiters want to network with you. They may be hoping you know someone with the qualifications that they desire. If they're legitimate recruiters, it may lead to something for you.

Don't give out the names of your friends or associates. If you want to make a referral, give the name of the employer to your friend to follow up on.

Social Media Services

*"Social media clearly is a significant phenomenon in today's world for both
general consumers and users up and down the age spectrum. Any social
media platform is worth examining. Social media expands business, develops
relationships, product innovation and service delivery — what an incredibly
powerful communication tool."*

— TOBY DAYTON, PRESIDENT AND CEO, LINKUP.COM

Social media sites continue to evolve. Some that are popular today may
be replaced by new technologies in the future. As social media sites are
playing an increasing role in the job search, it is important to keep up with
the latest technologies and how they can help you. Your local WorkForce
Center can help you stay current in terms of websites and other Web-based
resources that can assist your job search.

Social networking services such as LinkedIn and Facebook are Web-based
platforms that unite people with similar interests, tastes, passions and
communities. Facebook and Twitter, two of the most popular networks,
have really taken off in the last few years, mainly as a medium for people
to communicate with old friends and acquaintances. That role is steadily
evolving to include discussions and groups related to careers. LinkedIn, on
the other hand, focuses entirely on people in the business community.

In general, social networking services first ask you to create a "profile" that
has information about your interests and activities, career and education.
Once you have filled out a basic profile, you can search for people you know
using search tools provided by the service. You can request that certain people
become a part of your network, and they can accept or reject the offer.

If you are trying social networking for the first time, it's a good idea to start small. Log on, find friends and acquaintances, and begin sharing meaningful tidbits from your life or job search. Skip useless information about what you ate today or anything that doesn't add value to your job search. You can post photographs, links to articles, videos and other content related to your career or personal interest. These are far more valuable to your social network.

Job seekers can use social networking as a job search tool. Connecting through the Internet may relieve some of the stress of traditional face-to-face networking because it can be easier to communicate through a typed message than to call someone you don't know very well. When you make a networking connection in person, ask if they use a social networking service and would like to connect that way.

Social networks also offer a way for you to build your personal brand, a strategy discussed in Chapter 3. By having accounts on all major social media sites you can build an image for yourself as an expert in a field and an intriguing personality.

It's wise to keep your image on social networking sites professional. Some studies show as many as 80 percent of employers look at your social networking profiles to see how you act beyond the interview. Don't let this scare you away from using these tools since social networking services are a great way to create new contacts and keep in touch with old ones. Now, let's take a look at the most popular social media sites.

Facebook

Facebook is by far the largest social media platform, with 300 million users and counting. Primarily, Facebook connects friends and colleagues with one another and provides spaces for conversations, videos, photographs and, of course, profiles of users. More and more, Facebook has drifted into the business arena through the interest of users and through the development of third-party applications that assist in finding jobs.

One of those applications, "Advanced Search," allows a user to find profiles of people who attended a certain college, who once worked at a particular company or who live in your community. You can even search for people by location, age and first name — in case you've forgotten their surnames.

In an effort to get to know their job applicants, employers often look at Facebook accounts of applicants. In one CareerBuilder survey, 35 percent of companies reported not hiring someone because of what was found on a social networking site. It is wise to post only comments and images on Facebook and other social media sites that you would want your prospective boss to see.

LinkedIn

LinkedIn is a social networking site specifically for connecting with other business and individuals. It will be key to your social networking strategy because it deals with people in business looking for information about business. Founded in 2002 and launched in May 2003, LinkedIn had more than 42 million registered users in 200 countries by October 2009.

The network provides an important user base for job seekers, according to an Anderson Analytics 2008 survey, which found 66 percent of LinkedIn participants are decision makers. Of those, 16 percent are managers and 28 percent serve at the director/vice-president level or above.

Job seekers can establish a professional presence online by creating a resume, gaining recommendations and answering questions. There is also a job board that allows groups and businesses to post openings. The most important item to remember about LinkedIn is that simply creating a profile will not help you make the connections to find a job. You must interact and create valuable content and connections to resonate with employers and other members alike. For assistance learning how to use LinkedIn, there's a tutorial to help you at http://learn.linkedin.com/job-seekers/.

LinkedIn assists you in establishing connections with coworkers at past jobs, former managers, and your network of friends and acquaintances. You can use LinkedIn to remind them of your availability for employment and to share with them your insights on industries or events or information on business issues. Those members, in turn, can assist you in linking to members you may not know but who could have jobs in their businesses or be aware of openings elsewhere. It's also a good idea to join LinkedIn alumni, special interest and industry groups. They all have engaged members on the network and they sometimes discuss various job openings. Having connections won't get you the position, but joining groups and offering meaningful answers to questions will call attention to your expertise and showcase your value.

Twitter **twitter**

Twitter is a micro-blogging social media platform allowing members to follow one another and send messages no longer than 140 characters, or around two sentences. Politicians promote their ideas to constituents, news organizations give information about stories as they develop, celebrities keep fans updated on their lives, and regular folks reveal, well, anything they want, from their passions to what's up with their kids. The tweet, as a message is called, often refers to a longer article, video or photo gallery.

Twitter can enhance a job search in several ways, but savvy job seekers primarily use it as a networking tool. These short, real time messages provide a perfect electronic platform to let people know you are looking for a job — and to establish yourself as a valuable candidate for the jobs you seek. Take it from Barbara Maldonado, who told CNNMoney.com about her success using Twitter to network her way to a new job. "When I updated my status that I had been laid off, [a friend] referred me for a position that was open at his company, which is where I work now … Without actively participating in that discussion, I would not have made the contact for the job."

You could use Twitter to refer your followers to your LinkedIn page, to inform them you recently graduated from a college, or to tweet about things going on in your career. You can participate and impress employers and people in your network by linking to articles or grabbing relevant quotes on your industry. If you want to tweet a link to something, but the URL consumes most of your 140-character limit, use www.tinyurl.com to shorten the length.

As it stands today, Twitter is much easier to use as a networking tool than as a hub for job leads. However, new ways to find solid job leads on this medium are emerging every day. Check with your local WorkForce Center for up-to-date resources for conducting job searches on the Web.

Blogs

Short for weblog, blogs can be used for individuals, professionals, businesses, corporations or specific genres. Usually a more professional blog will have a specific focus, such as landscaping, architecture, engineering or fashion. Blogs offer the authors an opportunity to write "posts" — short pieces, generally, although some can go long when the topic demands that they share their thoughts or ideas. Posts feature photos, videos and text, and a place where visitors can interact by sending an e-mail message or even a video.

A series of posts about the same subject is called a "thread." You can join a conversation by commenting on a post or simply read what people are saying. If you choose to comment, you must be sure to keep it professional and related to the subject. Diverting from the subject or leaving inappropriate comments is considered poor "netiquette."

As with all social media, please be careful. Never post personal information online or work-related information. Some people have been "dooced," a coined term for losing one's job via blog comments. To avoid that fate, don't post personal or company information on your blog, even in a positive light. Use your blog to speak about industry trends or to highlight white papers, articles and other content you have produced regarding your profession, and remember to link them to your Facebook and Twitter accounts.

In terms of your job search, reading blogs is an effective way to get an "insider look" at various occupations, industries or fields. Reading a specific company's blog is a great way to expand your research. When interviewing, it is important to show that you are up to date on the happenings in your field of interest. Since many blogs are written by experts — self-proclaimed or otherwise — keep an eye out for good ones that will give you great insights into trends in your profession.

MINNESOTA JOB BLOGS

www.mnheadhunter.com

www.jobdig.com

http://blog.simplyhired.com/

http://iseekinteractive.org/blog/

NOTES

_____

_____

_____

_____

_____

_____

_____

_____

_____

_____

_____

_____

_____

_____

_____

_____

_____

_____

_____

_____

_____

_____

_____

CHAPTER 8

Facing Unemployment at 50 and Older

"The other day a man asked me what I thought was the best time of life. 'Why,' I answered without a thought, 'now.'"

— DAVID GRAYSON, AMERICAN JOURNALIST

Over 50 is far from over the hill. Some employers may quietly view older workers as technologically challenged, skeptical of the unknown and expensive. Of course, all of these attributes can be seen in younger workers as well, but they seem to be applied more often to workers beyond even 40 years old. Age discrimination is an issue that is growing louder as baby boomers move into their 50s and face obstacles they once thought were only reserved for their parents.

The AARP (formerly the American Association of Retired Persons) and RetirementJobs.com found in two studies in 2009 that 80 to 95 percent of respondents see "age bias as a fact of life." Even the federal Age Discrimination in Employment Act (ADEA) can't deny the reality that some employers consciously or subconsciously avoid hiring older workers.

Bob Skladany, an online columnist for the AARP.org website, notes: "While the ADEA makes age-based discrimination in hiring, pay, benefits, training, advancement and termination illegal, many people over 50, and increasingly older than 40, believe that age bias still exists and affects them."

But don't get discouraged. The website G060.com says older workers get new jobs at an annual rate of 4.1 percent — double the rate of the general population — and account for 22 percent of the nation's job growth despite being only 10 percent of its workforce. By 2015 the number of employees 55 and older will nearly double to more than 31 million.

The best approach to finding a job at any age is to face it head on and make changes as needed. The proverb "you're only as old as you feel" is applicable in job hunting; you want to recapture the energy of your youth and mix it with the toughness and experience of age. And you may want to adopt slightly different tactics from those used by younger workers in dealing with research, resumes and interviewing.

Research

Applying everywhere probably isn't going to work, if it ever did. Whenever you're networking or speaking to friends, family and acquaintances, ask if they know anyone in a position to hire, or more specifically, any employers who prefer hiring older workers. Networking is how most people find employment; older job seekers tend to know more people who have been working or are working than younger job seekers, which is a distinct advantage. In your community, it is likely that most companies care less about age and more about quality of work. Try to find out who they are and then begin making contacts.

There are several online resources available for older job seekers, in particular two sponsored by the AARP. One lists major national employers that abide by age-neutral policies and another lists employers recognized by the AARP for "exceptional practices" regarding older workers. Both can be found at www. aarp.org. Job boards worth checking out include Retirementjobs.com, which lists jobs and offers "Age Friendly Certification" to employers that are open to hiring older workers. Others include RetiredBrains.com, seniorjobbank.com, Jobs40.com, workforce50.com, yourencore.com, the AARP Message Board at Vault.com, Age Issues Message Board at Monster.com and Seniors4hire.org.

Resumes

Older workers who have had many positions and years of work could obviously fill up many pages of a resume. The temptation is to showcase your entire career to make the point that no one else applying has been in the trenches as long as you. Avoid this strategy at all costs.

A resume is not a history. It's a tactical, "living" tool to showcase how your skills and accomplishments make you the top candidate for the position/occupation you're applying for today.

Older workers should limit and focus their experience depending on what they are applying for. If it's a managerial job, go back 15 years; a technical job, 10 years; and a high-tech job, three years. You might place older jobs into the "Other Experience" category or eliminate them altogether.

Write a "functional" or "combination" resume that de-emphasizes your career chronology and emphasizes skills and accomplishments. List your employment history beneath that. You can cluster your skills under three or four headings/categories that you know are important to anyone working in the position you are applying for, such as leadership, teamwork, innovation, computer skills, communication skills, supervisory skills and so forth.

When writing your resume, it's OK to leave a few things out, especially irrelevant jobs you held in the distant past. List where you went to school and your degrees, not the years you received them. Emphasize your flexibility in the cover letter and on the resume. After all, you've spent "a few years" managing and adjusting to change.

Other key points to get across in the resume or cover letter: (1) your desire for a long-term position, (2) your solid attendance history, (3) your reliability and honesty, (4) your flexibility, (5) your ability to learn new skills, and (6) training and professional development courses and programs you have attended.

Computer skills are important in nearly all positions these days. Some employers may assume folks in mid-career lack these skills, so it's your job to dispel this myth early and clearly. List your computer software and technology-related skills as close to the top of Page 1 of your resume as possible. Go ahead and set up free LinkedIn, Twitter or other social media accounts and include these, along with your e-mail address, in your contact information at the top of Page 1.

If your resume is several years old, there is a good chance it needs a new format. Update your template! Remember to save it as both a plain text file for uploading to websites and as a Word file for physical distribution through the mail, or as an attachment.

Show you're up to date! Make sure the words in your resume reflect terminology that is currently used in your field. If you're uncertain about current terminology, you could do some research by reading industry publications, checking out association websites and, if you're not a member, joining a professional group.

The whole focus of an older worker's resume should be on matching skills and accomplishments with the open position, not a recap of a long career.

Cover Letters

Katherine Hansen, associate publisher of Quint Careers, says writing autobiographical letters that specify the number of years you have spent in a field can backfire. "Significant experience" works just as well.

Use a cover letter to accentuate your adaptability to new situations, your enthusiasm, your "willingness to learn," as well as your reputation as a proven talent and team player. The AARP says cover letters should be as short as half a page and mention who referred you to the job (if this is the case), two or three accomplishments from your career that would make a good impression and your strong interest in the position. Be self-confident but not too boastful or too desperate, the organization suggests.

Interviews

It's important to dress well and look sharp on the day of the interview.

As the questioning begins, always stress your skills and your experience. Stay away from starting any sentence with "when I was your age ..." or "this is how we used to do that. ..." Tell the interviewer you have significant problem-solving experience and would be happy to share your expertise with others. Hone in on a few examples revealing your prowess in getting things done.

Prior to entering the interview you should have updated your skills if necessary. As noted above, if the job requires computer skills, understanding the Microsoft Office suite, e-mail and any other relevant programs is very important. If an application that you have not used comes up during the conversation, express solidly your willingness and eagerness to learn. Have one or two stories or examples in mind about how you were able to quickly master a new skill or task to solve an employer's problem. The adage "show don't tell" is worth revisiting during job interviews. People like stories, not just a dry recitation of facts from a long and fruitful career.

It is illegal for the interviewer to ask your age, unless you are interviewing for certain jobs such as an airline pilot. If you are asked about your age, the AARP suggests you respond by saying, "How do you see my age affecting my ability to do the job?" Do so in a polite, conservational, not-angry tone.

Finally, if you get the interview and you're speaking to a contemporary around your age, your comfort level will grow. But keep on guard in sharing too much about your career or your personal life. Stick to the topic at hand.

A former newspaper boss recounts an excellent job candidate who lapsed into stories about her divorce. The interviewer felt a bit unnerved by the episode and worried that the same things could happen when she dealt with sources and with staff. After all, the interview only lasted an hour and he knew her entire life story.

Interviewees should not reveal details about their personal lives and should stay away from sharing gossip about people in their industries, even though they may think they're speaking to a confidante. When you've been in business for decades and you interview with a colleague, getting too chummy could backfire.

Remember, how you come across in an interview reveals your attitude — and to many employers, your attitude is just as important as your job skills when making an employment decision. Stay positive. Don't come across as a know-it-all, but do communicate that you can add value immediately.

Another issue in interviews is, of course, wages and benefits. Just because you have 30 years of experience doesn't mean you will receive more pay than a younger candidate.

Wages and Benefits

AARP columnist Bob Skladany recommends you study any offers closely, without a sense of desperation. Look at your employment status (contract or regular employee), pay, health benefits, secondary benefits (disability and/or life insurance), paid time off, retirement savings plans, work schedule and potential for growth. Ask for this information in writing, even though it isn't required of employers.

If you like the job, Skladany believes you should take it. If you have concerns, speak to the employer or recruiter while taking care not to ask too much.

CASE STUDY:
AN ENGINEER AND MARKETER

Tom Bjorgum says many employers are more than willing to overlook a few gray hairs if a job seeker has a world of good experience.

A Vietnam War veteran with a long career in engineering and marketing, Bjorgum, 59, lost his job at a motion automation company in 2008. He put together a chronological resume, worked the Internet job sites, networked through a job group at his church and hoped for the best.

When no offers came, Bjorgum received advice from a job search expert suggesting he write a skills-based resume, emphasizing his talent rather than career. He bought a resume software package and started over.

His new resume landed him an interview with a company that had posted a position on Monster.com. A week later, amazingly, he was sitting in an office entertaining a job offer from that company. (Bjorgum worked hard to improve his base salary, a strategy he describes in Chapter 10.)

The key to getting the job, he believes, was using a skills resume and only listing relatively recent jobs within the past 10 to 15 years, rather than his entire career. Having the rare combination of engineering and marketing helped.

"I felt I was in the driver's seat at the end, especially when I interviewed with the president of the company, and I felt there was a sense of urgency to get someone hired," he says. "I had good timing."

If the salary appears too low, first ask if the employer will entertain a counterproposal and then request a minimum of a 10 percent bump due to your expertise or experience. The employer has the right to say no, leaving you with the uncomfortable decision of whether to take it or leave it, he says. The key is to try for an improved contract that is "meaningful."

Negotiating for higher hourly wages is possible in the skilled trades, personal services, administrative and clerical areas, he says, but basic benefits are unlikely to be changed. You can ask for flexibility in scheduling and more training. For professional, salaried positions the opportunity for a higher salary, deferred compensation, incentive pay, stock options and other benefits is much higher. When vying for these jobs insist on a written employment agreement. Senior professional and upper management jobs offer the greatest negotiating opportunity on every aspect of employment.

Other Options

It might be time to look at other options for your career path. This could mean embarking on a new career or self-employment. Starting your own business is a dream of many who never had an opportunity until becoming unemployed. You could start your dream business, buy an existing one or enlist in a franchise program. Each of these career paths has an enviable advantage in that the only person who can fire you is yourself. The strategy comes, too, with a high failure rate.

An absolute requirement of the approach is that you will have to become an entrepreneur. You will have to find and nurture clients, manage business partners and staff, network, research, learn new skills and be a self-starter. Self-discipline is a necessity.

On the whole, the traits needed for exploring these options sound a lot like the activity involved in finding a job, don't they? Halfway through a job search you might decide to buy or start a business, grow one or become a consultant.

The leap toward consulting from job hunting isn't all that much of a stretch, especially since many job seekers consult while they look for jobs. Some even stop trying to find a job because they have become successful consultants and like the flexibility. They sometimes even surpass their previous salaries and can logoff early for a game of tennis, a bike ride or family needs.

Millions of Americans have found some satisfaction and success by going off on their own. It is still the American dream. It is not easy. It is not without real challenges, such as the cost of health insurance. Still, in a time when it can seem like no one will hire you, there is one person who can hire you — yourself. It may be a time to go for it.

PROFILE:

JOSEPH SCHUFMAN, SALES EXECUTIVE, ISOFT

Joseph Schufman lost his job at Verizon when he was 63, an age when many people decide to retire.

Schufman, though, wasn't ready to retire just yet. The company gave him a generous severance package along with a non-compete contract that said he could not work for a year for any company directly competing against Verizon. Despite the breathing room of severance and the non-compete year, he wasted little time in laying the groundwork for a new job.

First, he opened shop as a consultant, working a day a week. He networked constantly, often leaving his home for 7:30 a.m. coffee with people in business. He tried to reach two people a day and get two more contacts from them.

"That was my self-imposed quota, and most people, I found, are willing to help you," he says.

He created a lengthy LinkedIn.com account and an eFolioMinnesota website, both describing his career in detail. After sending out several resumes, he discovered he had to tailor a version for each job or at least each occupation emphasizing the skills the job required. His resume dropped from 3½ pages to two.

"You have to write the resume for the job and not send a generalized one," he says.

Two offers finally came through, both from networking contacts — one at AT&T and the other at ISoft, where he now works. The company came away impressed when he described the vast network of contacts that he could tap for sales.

Schufman sees that age bias is a problem, but he says he's helped by a youthful disposition and positive attitude. "Everyone I interviewed with was younger than me," he says. "There's just no getting around your age. You just have to deal with it and not draw attention to it."

CHAPTER 9

The Job Interview

"Success is where preparation and opportunity meet."

— BOBBY UNSER, FORMER INDY 500 CHAMPION

So you've come to that cherished moment in your job search when your hard work has paid off and you received the call to come in for an interview. Now is the time for yet more preparation. You will have to brush up on the employer by doing research, start a list of anticipated questions, and practice answering questions and interviewing.

You will have to make your personal appearance a priority and get into a mentally alert frame of mind before walking into an interview room to face someone who might be your manager someday.

You have to look smart, think smart and be ready. Star cyclist Lance Armstrong once said he and his team prepared so well for the Tour de France that there were few surprises they had not considered while training. And Benjamin Franklin probably offered the best summation for anyone pursuing a goal in life: "By failing to prepare, you are preparing to fail."

Interview Preparation

Knowing the kind of information the employer is likely to seek will help you prepare for the interview. Employers want to know your motivation for employment, your ability to do the job, how you will fit into the organization and how much you will cost them. Being able to answer probing questions in these areas will make for a successful interview. And being able to ask good questions and look for opportunities to show off your knowledge of the company you're interviewing with can make all the difference in the world.

A great advantage is to have as much information as you can about the position before that first interview. It will help you to target your skills to the specific needs of the employer and demonstrate your enthusiasm for the job. Companies, after all, have limited information from which to make a decision — an application or resume, references and perhaps a brief interview. It's up to YOU to convince the employer you are the best person for the job. Be prepared to relate your career, training and education to what the hiring manager desires in a new hire.

Prior to walking in the door, you should cover a few of the following areas on your own.

Do Your Research

When on the phone arranging your interview, do a little interviewing yourself. Ask about the interview process, who you will be interviewing with (one person or a panel) and how long it will take. Ask if you can see the full job description again and inquire if the company needs any supporting documentation. Get the address of the interview location (companies have multiple sites, and going to the wrong one is a major slip up) and the office and cell phone number of the interviewer just in case you blow a tire on the freeway on the way there.

On your own, study the company's website, brochures, annual business reports, trade periodicals, manufacturer's guides and any other materials you can find. Good sources for finding that information were covered in Chapter 2, but generally the three spots are libraries, Minnesota WorkForce Centers and the Internet.

Match Your Skills to the Job

Once you've gathered what you need to know about the employer, look at the job description again and study how your skills, experience and employment history match what the company requests. By coupling your strengths with their list of desired traits, you might be halfway there — well, you must be, or they would not have asked you for the interview.

If you're deficient in an area, you must be ready to convince the employer you can and will learn the skill. You could also show how your other skills will make up for this weakness or have non-work examples of the trait, such as being a volunteer leader of a nonprofit group or committee. Another strategy is to have a plan of action to overcome the deficiency. Don't have Web design skills? Knowing when and where you can enroll in a Web design course in your community may convince the employer you're the right person to hire.

Find Your Attitude

Employers are looking for people with a positive work attitude. Often employers emphasize attitude over skills, training and experience. Look for ways to show your enthusiasm for the job, willingness to learn, spirit of cooperation and respect for the employer. Review your skills for reinforcement of your qualifications. Rehearse how you'll present yourself. Be positive, truthful and realistic.

Athletes call it their "game face." And make sure to have it for the interview, says Letetia Klebel, human resources manager of Pro Fabrication in Madison,

Minn. Klebel says she sees many people who haven't interviewed in 15 years. She suggests coming in with a good attitude, and try to be relaxed. And be willing and able to ask questions. "I can't believe how many people come in for professional jobs and don't have any questions for us," says Klebel. "You should always come prepared with a couple of questions to ask us about the company and our jobs."

Look Good

An important part of the impression you make on an employer is your physical appearance. An employer might reason that the person who doesn't care about her/his appearance won't care about the job. Neat, clean and conservative is a safe standard for dress and grooming. No matter what kind of job you are applying for you should look as professional as possible. You may not be applying for a job that requires a suit, but for the interview you may want to try to be, for a day, the best-dressed person to visit the employer's office or plant. Here's an introduction on looking good:

Get a good night's sleep

Take a shower the morning of the interview

Shave

Brush your teeth

Comb your hair

Clean your fingernails

Wear clean and pressed clothes

Wear proper clothes for the job

Conceal body piercings

Clean and shine your shoes

Avoid smoking before the interview

Do not chew gum during an interview

Do not wear sunglasses

Types of Interviews

The purpose of an interview is to get acquainted and to learn about one another. Employers evaluate your qualifications, and you get to provide a human face to a resume and a phone call, as well as sell the employer on your skills, experience and enthusiasm. But the interview is not just about you; it's also about them. It is an opportunity for you to learn more about the job — what it is really like — and find out if you really want it. Moreover, you will discover whether this is a company you will enjoy working for.

Three common types of interviews are telephone screening, in-person screening and the selection interview. It doesn't matter what type of interview you face; what matters is that you present your qualifications to the final decision maker while maintaining good relations with everyone you come into contact with, from the staff at the waiting area to receptionists and parking lot attendants. If you're lucky, you may see them all again when you get the job.

INTERVIEW CLOTHING TIPS FOR WOMEN

Either pants, suits or skirted suits are appropriate. Skirt length should be at or just below the knee. Make sure your clothing is not too tight and avoid cleavage and excessive perfume. Keep make-up and nail polish simple and conservative, jewelry conservative and minimal. Wear clean, low-heeled shoes and stay away from faddish clothing.

INTERVIEW CLOTHING TIPS FOR MEN

Make sure your belt matches your shoes, keep facial hair neatly trimmed and match a decent tie to your suit or sports coat. Comb your hair neatly, wear dress shoes and don't smell like a cologne ad.

Telephone Screening Interview

This interview saves the employer time by eliminating candidates based on essential criteria such as employment objective, education or required skills. Since these interviews will often occur unexpectedly, it's important your job search records are organized and kept where you can reach them at a moment's notice. If you are unprepared, simply ask if you can call back in five minutes, or have them call back. It's not an unreasonable demand, and the employer may be impressed that you seek to be prepared instead of just winging the interview.

In-person Screening Interview

The company can verify your qualifications for the position and establish a preliminary impression of attitude, interest and professional style. A professional screener from the employer's human resources department most often conducts the interview. At this stage, the goal is to select candidates to meet with the decision maker. You still have to perform well during the interview and leave a good impression.

Selection Interview

Conducted by the decision maker, this interview will probe your qualifications and assess your comfort level with the challenges of the position and other team members. There may be more than one interview at this stage. As the candidates are whittled down, you may be invited back to speak with the same person and with other managers or members of a work group. Your ability to establish rapport and present yourself as the right person is critical.

Even with just one interviewer, opinions of the others will be sought and may have an effect on the outcome. When you're invited to interview with a number of people, it's important to present yourself effectively to each one of them. Remember, they will be evaluating your skills and ability to fit in. As always, be yourself, but sell to each person's concerns.

Behavioral Interview

Traditional interview questions, such as "tell me about yourself," offer employers limited information about your qualifications. Behavioral interviewing can provide more information about your on-the-job behavior, personality and character. The interviewer will ask questions that require you to describe how you have handled work-related situations. For instance, a question might be: "Describe a time when you had to overcome a stressful work situation and how you dealt with it." From an employer's perspective, behavioral interviewing gives more insight about your potential than traditional questions.

Sometimes this technique is called STAR, which stands for "Situation, Task, Action and Results." That's the order you will follow should you encounter an interviewer who uses the STAR method. It's a good idea to think of a few STAR stories ahead of time that you can adapt to different behavioral interviewing questions. Remember the importance of being authentic and real. Don't say anything like, "Well, I never had the kind of problems in my past job that you want me to address here." The interviewer will know that is unlikely.

Take it as a chance to tell a story that illustrates your skills and offers the interviewer insights that give a good impression of you. As you tell your STAR stories, employers will listen for evidence of the skills required for the job. By now you've done plenty of research about the position, and the STAR method allows you to show employers you possess the skills they need.

Work Sample Interview

This type of interview gives applicants an opportunity to show what they have done at previous jobs. It could be the place for graphic artists to display portfolios and salespeople to make a sales presentation. (Even better, do as one job expert suggests, and bring potential sales leads to the interview!) An office worker may be asked to complete a business letter using a specific type of computer software program. An editor might be asked to edit a document.

Peer Group Interview

This is an opportunity to meet and talk with your prospective coworkers. Just as in other interviews, the peer group will be evaluating you, determining how you fit in.

Group Interview

This type of interview takes place with a group of other candidates, and usually more than one interviewer. Introduce yourself to other candidates and, of course, be polite. Try to show confidence by volunteering to respond first to a few questions, but do not dominate the entire interview. To show your ability to be a team player, compliment another candidate's response and then build on it with your own thoughts. Direct your answer to the individual asking the question, but try to maintain some eye contact with the other members of the group. Don't forget to smile.

Luncheon or Coffee Interview

This type of interview assesses how well you can handle yourself in a social situation. Employer representatives may include the hiring manager, a human resource department member and one or more peer employees. Choose your meal selection carefully. Spilling on your blouse or tie isn't likely to make a favorable impression. Select healthy and easy things to eat so you can answer questions and pay attention to the conversation.

If the interview is conducted at a coffee shop — and a fair number of interviews are these days — the setting probably has more to do with the hiring manager than anything else. He or she wants to escape the office and speak to you in a casual, informal atmosphere that will likely make for an honest discussion of your strengths and weaknesses. Try not to consider if others are listening in — they probably are — and use the time to reveal your commitment to the industry and your desire to work for the company.

Stress Interview

A stress interview re-creates some challenging situations you might run into on the job. The interviewer asks you a number of tough questions that are designed to make you somewhat uncomfortable. For example, he or she might present a job-related scenario and ask you to explain how you would respond. Keep your cool, take your time in responding to the questions and reward yourself when it's all over. Don't take it personally. This is usually a test of whether you can handle stress on the job and can assess a complicated question quickly.

Video Conference Interview

Some employers today use video conferences to conduct meetings or carry out other aspects of their business, such as interviewing candidates who live in other states or communities a good distance from where they are located. Conducting an interview via video conference enables an employer to save travel costs and still have, in effect, a person-to-person interview. If the thought of facing a camera during an interview frightens you, practice video conferencing beforehand or in front of a mirror.

Communicate Your Best Image

Get everything organized early. Fill out applications neatly, completely and in black ink. If requested, collect letters of recommendation, your reference list, copies of licenses, driving record (for those jobs that require it) and Social Security or alien card. Bring a notebook, pen, business cards and extra copies of your resume. Bring your portfolio, and if you have a Web-based version, write down the URL so you can find it rapidly.

And put it all in a nice briefcase. Look professional.

Arrive on time for the interview. Plan your schedule and route so you arrive 10 to 15 minutes prior to the appointment time. Do not — repeat, do not — arrive a half hour early or an hour early to show your desire for the job. Your interviewers are likely to find this irritating because they may have to change their schedule to handle your earlier arrival. They gave you an interview time for a reason, and show up a few minutes before it, and no more.

While you are sitting in the lobby, review questions you want to ask in the interview, your resume and your personal data record for related skills. By now you should have convinced yourself you are the best person for the job. Now it's time to convince the employer.

Send Good Signals

The vast majority of communication is nonverbal. Your posture, walk, dress, facial movement, energy, gestures and eye contact are all nonverbal signals. Try using a natural greeting and shake hands firmly, but only if a hand is offered to you first. Show reserved confidence and let the interviewer start the dialogue.

Focus on the questions and answer carefully. When your chance comes ask good questions about the job, the company and the team you may be joining.

Every interview is a learning experience. Use each one as a building block for the next one. You may go through many interviews before you connect with the right job. You should get better with practice. Analyze what went right and what went wrong with every interview, and then ensure that the surprise question or the strange inquiry during the next one does not throw you off course.

Show and Tell

You may be a good worker, but you have to back up statements with samples of your productivity in past jobs. Tell employers about your skills, because no one else will. Let employers know you can adjust, work well with others, and fit into a new environment without complaints. Tell a story from your experience that illustrates your flexibility.

Stories are important. "When you interview, tell stories. You know you're going to encounter the question, 'What are your strengths?' Don't give a list," writes Penelope Truck in "Brazen Careerists." "It's not persuasive. Tell a story about your strengths. This way you tell the hiring manager something memorable and you get in a bit about your achievements."

You should emphasize your commitment to learning. Demonstrate this through your own independent study, professional development, education, workshops and awards. Your plan for future development also communicates your commitment to learning.

Finish Strong

Demonstrate interest by asking when the position will be filled. In the final stage, summarize why you're qualified by stating strengths and qualities you may have forgotten to emphasize earlier. Remember, don't overstay your time.

Ask what the next step is in the hiring process. Will there be additional interviews? When will the hiring decision be made? When could you call back for the decision? Be proactive in your follow-up. Schedule the next interview. Arrange to call the employer to learn the decision.

Follow-up

Evaluate the interview. What went well in the interview? How can you improve?

Record your follow-up plans. Write the date and time for your next contact with the employer. Be sure you follow through on these plans.

Send thank you letters, notes or e-mails within 24 hours to each person with whom you interviewed. For information on thank you letters and notes, see the next chapter entitled Finishing Touches.

Key Interview Questions

Employers use all kinds of interview strategies. We will look at typical questions and then delve into those that require more attention to storytelling and detail, and the ones that tease out valuable clues about how you would fit into a work environment.

Can you tell me about yourself?

This is an open-ended question often asked to help break the ice in the interview. The important thing to remember is to keep the answer job-related. Your response to this question should last about two minutes and be especially well-practiced.

Why are you interested in working for this company?

This will show the employer you've done your homework. State the positive things you've learned about the company and how they fit with your career goals. Mention you just read an article or saw a piece on the news about the company. Highlight that you were impressed by the performance of a particular unit, or the entire company, over the past year. "Your sales increase of 20 percent was impressive," goes a long way toward showing you did your research.

Can you tell me about your education?

Even though your resume includes this information, some employers want you expand on the subject. Mention your grade point if it was over 3.0 and what impact your education has had on your understanding of the world and of your professional field. Always note the classes, seminars, workshops and on-the-job training you've attended that support your job goals.

Why have you chosen this particular field?

This is one way to show your enthusiasm and dedication to your career. Share your continued excitement to be a nurse, or a technologist, or a teacher or a truck driver.

Can you describe your best and worst bosses?

This could be a trap. Don't present a negative picture of any past employers. If given a choice, always talk about your best boss. If pressed to describe the worst boss, pick a work-related characteristic that can be stated in a positive way. For example, "I had a supervisor who was vague when issuing assignments. I learned to ask questions so that I knew what was expected."

In a job, what interests you the most and the least?

This will give the employer another gauge for measuring how well you will fit the job opening.

What is your major weakness?

"I have none" won't work or will come off as less than honest. Turn the question into a positive by stating how you overcame a weakness. Martin Yate, author of "Knock 'em Dead, the Ultimate Search Guide," gives an illustration where a job seeker admits to not always handling paperwork well. His manager tells him to work on getting the paperwork in order. He "takes it to heart" and changes his behavior and notes, "You only have to tell me something once." The scenario, adds Yate, offers you the added bonus of "showing that you accept and act on criticism."

Can you give an example of how you solved a problem in the past?

It's important to be able to show the process you go through when presented with a problem. State the problem and the steps you followed to reach the solution. If it's hard to come up with a problem, switch to a project and how you completed it.

What are your strengths?

This is the time to describe the skills you've identified that will most effectively "market" you as an employee. Offer a confident and measured response, delineating skills or skill sets and how they have led to your success in past jobs and will benefit another employer in the future.

How do others describe you?

Another way for the employer to ask this would be, "How would you fit into this work group?" If you aren't comfortable with this question or don't know how to answer it, call some friends or people you've worked with and ask them to describe you.

What do you consider the most important idea you contributed or your most noteworthy accomplishment in your last job?

Give examples of ways in which you saved the employer time or money, or developed an office procedure that improved efficiency. Any leadership opportunities should be illuminated.

Where do you see yourself in three years?

Telling the interviewer "In your job!" isn't a good idea. Do indicate that you hope to acquire sufficient skills and knowledge within that time to make a positive contribution to the company. You might pick a position a step or two above the post you are applying for, but tell the interviewer you only want a promotion you have earned and one in which you will have the confidence to succeed.

How do you think you will fit into this operation?

This is the time to express your interest in the job and knowledge of the employer. The more you know about the operation the easier this question will be to answer.

If you were hired, what ideas/talents could you contribute to the position or our company?

This is another great opportunity for you to sell your skills. By giving examples of past accomplishments, you help the employer visualize your contribution to the company.

Can you give an example where you showed leadership and initiative?

Even if you haven't had the title of lead worker, supervisor or manager, give examples of when you recognized a job needed to be done and you did it. Again, use samples outside the workforce if they fit.

Give me an example of when you were able to contribute to a team project?

Any job that requires communicating with others usually requires some amount of teamwork. For example, teamwork is used in sales because both parties have to state their needs and expectations before negotiating the sale. Families, community activities and school all require teamwork.

What have you done to develop or change in the last few years?

This shows a willingness to be challenged and to improve. Employers are looking for people who are willing to continue learning. Talk about formal and informal educational opportunities you've pursued. Mention books and periodicals you've read related to your field of interest.

Do you have any questions for me?

By asking questions, you again show interest in the job. Listed later in this chapter are some questions you may want to ask at your interview.

Keep your answers brief and job-related. Focus on your skills.

The Toughest Questions

Give direct, honest answers. Take your time. Develop the answer in your head before you respond. If you don't understand a question, ask for it to be repeated or clarified. You don't have to rush, but don't be indecisive.

Ask questions in return.

Be prepared. Answering difficult questions that may reflect negatively on you can be answered by using the "sandwich model." This model has a positive statement followed by admitting the negative situation, and ending with another positive statement about what you've done to overcome the problem. Ending with a positive statement leaves a positive impression. Anticipate tough questions and practice interviewing beforehand.

Why were you let go?

Try a few of these examples as a tactic to answering this hardest of questions.

My skills are in engineering (or name your field). My employer decided those skills were no longer needed. Therefore, I've taken some training and upgraded my skills (specify) to meet the qualifications for this type of job.

Or, if you were fired, career expert and columnist Joyce Lain Kennedy suggests several great answers, among them the following.

- I was cut loose and that was a blessing because I got a chance to explore different opportunities like the one we're talking about right now.

- My competencies weren't a good match with my former employer's needs.

- The job simply wasn't working out for my boss and me, and we both agreed it was time to move on.

- The former job was a learning experience, and I'm wiser now and want a chance to prove it.

- A new manager came in and cleaned house, including me, and I figured it was time to move on, anyway.

- Certain personal problems that I have surmounted upset my work life. I'm now up and running strong to exceed expectations in a new job. I wanted to move my career in a different direction and that set up the conditions for departure.

- I usually hit it off with bosses, but this time was an exception. We didn't hit it off and I'm not sure why.

- My job was offshored to India. I outlasted several downsizings but not the last one.

- I was desperate for work and took the wrong job.

"Keep it brief, keep it honest and keep it moving," she suggests.

ASKING QUESTIONS IN INTERVIEWS

When Karen Oldenborg went for an interview with the St. Francis School District in 2010, she had a couple of ideas of how to deal with tough questions.

She'd ask them herself.

In an interview for an administrative post in the district, Oldenborg asked a panel of school officials what weakness they saw in her resume. "You don't have a lot of experience in tracking things," one school official noted.

Oldenborg, 47, responded this way: "That's a good point. But I have learned multiple computer systems over the years and I am not afraid to jump in. When I have an issue with a system I only will ask you once."

At the end of the interview, the panel asked Oldenborg if she had any questions. "Yes, I have six," she said, before proceeding to ask about her duties, an average day on the job and other "process-related" inquiries.

"They looked at me with that 'oh, this is going to take a while,'" Oldenborg recalls with a laugh. She also asked panel members to spell their names so she could send each of them a thank you card.

As it turns out, the gesture wasn't necessary. Four hours after the interview, a school district official called and offered her the job, and nine months of unemployment finally ended.

It appears you haven't worked in the last five years or 10 years. Why?

I've been busy going to school full time (specify), raising two children and managing my home. Doing that on a daily basis gave me a lot of skills we generally don't acknowledge, like leadership, time management, teaching, coordination, planning and so forth.

I needed to address some health issues. It would not have been fair to an employer if I took too much time off from work. I'm now ready to return to work and give you 100 percent.

Why haven't you worked in the past 10 years?

I was trained in machine operation while at a correctional facility. I have now completed my GED and am ready to work for you.

Questions to Ask in an Interview

- Would you describe an average day on this job?
- What is the history of the position? Why is it vacant?
- What aspects of this job would you like to see performed better?
- What are the key challenges or problems of this position?
- Can the duties of this position be expanded?
- Where can I go from here, assuming I meet/exceed the job responsibilities?
- How would you describe the ideal candidate?
- What are the employer's short- and long-range objectives?
- What are some outside influences that affect company growth?
- Where does the company excel? What are its limitations?
- When and how will I be evaluated? What are the performance standards?
- With whom would I be working? Who would be my supervisor? Who would I supervise?
- What is the department's environment like?
- When will you make the hiring decision? May I call you for the decision? When is a good time?

Illegal and Legal Questions

Questions asked in an interview should focus on your qualifications for the job. Federal and state laws help ensure you aren't asked illegal questions, but occasionally they do come up on an application or in an interview. Some employers may not have a clear understanding of federal and state rules and inquire into areas that are legally off limits.

Questions should be job-related and not used to find out personal information. Employers should not ask about any of the following, because to not hire a candidate because of any one of them is discriminatory:

- Race
- Color
- Sex
- Religion
- National origin
- Birthplace
- Age
- Disability
- Marital/family status
- Genetic information

Illegal Questions

For the candidate, it's a good idea to have a plan of action ready if illegal job interview questions are ever asked. Think through possible illegal questions ahead of time and decide how you will handle them.

If you encounter illegal questions, you can be prepared to respond. You are attempting to determine why the interviewer is asking such a question. If you know the intent of the question, then you can reply with an appropriate answer. For example, if you are asked whether you are a United States citizen (not legal to ask), reply that you are authorized to work in the U.S., which is a question the employer can ask you and which is appropriate to answer.

Federal laws such as the Civil Rights Act and the Americans With Disabilities Act, as well as state law, prohibit the following questions:

- Do you prefer to go by Miss, Mrs. or Ms.?
- What is your maiden name?
- What is your native language and the language you speak at home?
- What is your ancestry?
- How many children do you have?
- Do you plan to have more children?
- How do you plan to care for your children while on the job?
- What is or was your spouse's name or line of work?
- What is your religion?
- Have you ever filed a workers' compensation claim or been injured on the job?
- Do you have any physical impairments that would prevent you from performing the job for which you're applying?
- Have you ever been arrested?
- What is your hair/eye color? What is your height/weight?
- Have you ever been hospitalized? If so, for what condition?
- Have you ever been treated by a psychiatrist or psychologist? If so, for what condition?
- Is there any health-related reason you may not be able to perform the job for which you're applying?
- How many days were you absent from work because of illness last year?
- Are you taking any prescribed drugs?
- Have you ever been treated for drug addiction or alcoholism?

Resources

Most illegal questioning is not deliberate. However, any individual who believes that his or her employment rights have been violated may file a charge of discrimination with the EEOC or the Minnesota Department of Human Rights by contacting:

> Equal Employment Opportunity Commission
> www.eeoc.gov
> (612) 335-4040
>
> Minnesota Department of Human Rights
> www.humanrights.state.mn.us
> (651) 296-5663

Perfectly Legal Questions

You can expect to hear one or more of the following questions, which are perfectly legal. In other parts of this book and this chapter, we address difficult questions that pose challenges, especially if you are an ex-felon looking for a chance to right your life.

- What is your current address and phone contact?
- Describe your education.
- What experience qualifies you for this job?
- Do you have licenses/certifications for this job?
- Are you willing to travel?
- What name(s) are your work records under?
- Are you available for overtime?
- Do you have the legal right to work in the United States?
- Have you served in the U.S. armed forces?
- Do you have any convictions other than misdemeanors?

OTHER INFORMATION EMPLOYERS CAN REQUEST

- Employers are required to verify that you are legally able to work in the United States before you start work. A current state photo ID card with a valid Social Security card usually meets this requirement. If you are not a citizen, be prepared to provide your Permanent Resident Card or other proof that you can work in this country.

- Physical exam and drug testing

DISCLOSING A DISABILITY

Deciding when or if you should disclose a disability can be a difficult decision. You should consult with an employment counselor or rehabilitation counselor at your local WorkForce Center if you have concerns about disclosing your disability.

As a general rule, if you will need an accommodation to participate in the job interview you should let the employer know this when the interview is scheduled. For example, if you are unable to use stairs, you might say, "I can't use stairs. I would appreciate it if you could hold the interview in a first-floor room or in a room that I can get to by elevator."

If you can do the job without accommodations, there is usually no need to disclose. If you know you will need reasonable accommodations, it is usually better to wait until after the job offer to discuss this.

If you realize after you start the job that you will need an accommodation to be successful, you should request this before your job performance is impacted.

Reasons You Didn't Get Hired

Usually people don't get hired due to a simple reality: For that job the employer found someone more qualified or who met certain specifications you didn't possess. Sometimes it is as simple as that. Don't beat up yourself too badly if everything seemed to have gone right. It may have. It just went better for someone else.

While the preceding reason is most common, here are a few other reasons people do not get hired: inability to express skills and information clearly, lack of interest and enthusiasm, lack of confidence and poise, over-aggressiveness, too much emphasis on money, poor personal appearance, unwillingness to start at the bottom, or lack of tact and courtesy.

It is reasonable to seek feedback from the employer about why you did not land the job, particularly if you went far in the interview process. That information can help you hone your job interview skills for next time.

CHAPTER 10

Finishing Touches

"Silent gratitude isn't much use to anyone."

— G.B. STERN, NOVELIST

Every job search needs finishing touches — those often overlooked actions likely to impress potential employers even if you don't get the job this time around. They show an attention to detail, an admirable and non-irritating persistence, and a genuine civility beyond just trying to use contacts and interviewers to find employment.

Applied regularly and teamed with appropriate skills and qualifications, a graceful finishing touch should eventually lead employers to see you as a potential hire, worthy of a second look and perhaps a job offer.

Just as accountants take the time to scrutinize their work one last time, job seekers should write thank you letters and other correspondences to continue their sales campaigns to land jobs.

A thoughtful note gives you one last chance to leave an outstanding and memorable impression on the employer. If done correctly, these steps can put you a cut above the competition. It shows initiative and care to complete the sales process, so to speak, even though potential employers may not see it precisely in that way. You should see it that way because finding a job, in the end, is all about selling you.

Post-Interview Steps

After spending all that time preparing for an interview and successfully sailing through it, do not drop the ball in the final hours. Here's a simple two-part approach that will take little time and yield great benefits by leaving an unmistakably good impression.

Contacting References

If your interview went well, you should contact your references to prepare them for a potential phone call or e-mail from the employer. You might recap the interview briefly to each reference and highlight any points you made that they can verify, or emphasize, should they be asked by the interviewer for a testimony to your skills, experience and character.

You might end up saying something like this to a reference: "Jim, the company seemed really interested in the management skills I provided for the business development projects we worked on from 2006 to 2008. If asked, could you elaborate and stress the important role I had during that time? You may recall it was a small team. No one volunteered to manage the projects except me, and they all turned out pretty successful."

It should be a given that references will agree with your point of view. If you have to persuade them, make sure they agree, in the end, with your perceptions. References can say the same good things about you, but you should remind them with an example or two of the kinds of qualities you possess.

During the interview, if you mentioned strong communication skills, then have one of your references highlight that trait and point to a project in which your writing and speaking skills were exercised to a good end. If you showed up at work on time, always did what was told, always pitched in when needed, then a reference should be able to back you up on those traits.

Thank You Notes, E-mails and Letters

Saying "thank you" in your job search isn't only an effective job search strategy, it's the right thing to do. Every thank you note or letter is an opportunity to sell your qualifications again. Sending a card or letter after an interview is common, but don't spare your thank you notes during the job hunt. Express your gratitude to employment contacts, members of your network and references who have extended themselves on your behalf, from informational interviewers to those who offer referrals or information.

Thank you may be said in person, by phone, an informal note, in a typed letter or by e-mail. Overall, handwritten notes work best because they are the most personal form of communication unless your handwriting tends to be sloppy. If you want to add a little style without having to write a thank you, try a less formal typeset in offering your acknowledgment.

The thank you note may be a simple handwritten card. The thank you letter, in contrast, should follow a standard business letter format. The situation and your personal style will determine which one you send.

POINTS TO CONSIDER

- Write a thank you letter or note no later than 24 hours after the interview. Be brief and to the point.

- Thank you notes, whether handwritten or electronic, must be clear, concise and legible.

- Include your personal business card if you have one.

- If there are multiple people, such as a panel interview, send a separate thank you to each person, or send a single thank you to a key person for distribution. When sending more than one thank you letter, personalize each one.

- When thanking a potential employer, restate your interest in the position and the employer.

- Always plan your follow-up. Make it a point to indicate when and how you will be following up.

- Say thank you when you're with the individual and follow up with a thank you note, letter, e-mail or phone call.

At the minimum, a thank you note or letter should be sent after all interviews. This is your chance to make one more impression before the decision is made. Send a thank you note even if you're turned down for a job. Let employers know you appreciate their consideration, and you'd be interested in future opportunities.

Some people may wonder if an e-mail is too impersonal for a thank you. Write both types of notes if you're really interested in getting the job. Craft a brief e-mail after the interview and then drop a thank you card to the company within 24 hours. Try not to be too overly enthusiastic in your thanks. Be professional, express your continued interest in the job and in working for the company, and mention your appreciation for the interview.

If You Get Turned Down

Upon receiving a phone call or letter of rejection, let interviewers know that although you're disappointed you're still interested in working for the employer. That is, if you are. If you are only marginally attracted to the company, be honest with yourself and do not follow up with the interviewer with any "still love to work with you" communications. But thank him or her for the consideration, of course.

Should you still have desires to work for the employer, thank the interviewer for the time and interest, re-emphasize your interest in openings and ask if you could continue to maintain contact. Find out if there are, or might be, other openings or other people you could contact.

Many times the person selected ends up turning down the job or doesn't work out. Keep the communication line open, positive and professional. This keeps your name in their mind for the next opening.

Stay positive. Congratulate yourself. You did get the interview, which means the employer was interested in you. Learn from the experience. Ask for feedback from the interviewer on what you could improve or do differently.

Keep trying. This isn't the time to stop. Forge ahead. Don't despair. Getting turned down happens to all of us at some point in our lives. It's up to you to decide which tips will work best for you.

The Salary Negotiation

Let's say your first interview with a prospective employer leads to further discussions. Congratulations. You are moving ahead in the process. Next you may face additional interviews and, inevitably, a conversation about compensation.

If an employer asks how much you expect to be compensated, give a salary range instead of a definite number. Come to the interview prepared with knowledge of a reasonable salary range for the position. Use a career information website to learn about the salary range for related positions. Otherwise, contacting the personnel office or a networking contact that works in the company may be helpful.

Let the employer bring up salary first and try to avoid the issue entirely in the initial interview. Delaying salary negotiation as long as possible allows you to better understand what the position entails before the question of salary is addressed. It also gives you more time to articulate what you'll bring to the employer before an offer is made.

The next step is salary negotiation. It can set the tone for your work life and experience with the employer. These are some suggestions to consider when you receive a job offer. Negotiating is a two-way street. Try to achieve a win-win situation. It's up to you to decide which tips will work best for you.

When You Get the Job

Should you get the job, congratulate yourself and then look closely at the offer you are receiving. If the job is a good fit and the salary and benefits meet your expectations, you may be inclined to accept it. On the other hand, if you think the salary is too low or the benefits are not quite right, you can negotiate for a better contract.

You may not get it, and you could run the risk of losing the opportunity. But many employers anticipate that some applicants will advocate for a stronger compensation package.

Negotiating Tips

Randall S. Hansen, a job negotiation expert, urges you to know the salary you can reasonably accept and expect, based on your experience and education and on industry wage standards. Some online sources, such as www.salary.com, can help you determine the salaries in certain jobs and fields based on years of experience. Never attend a job negotiation without knowing the average salary range in your field and at the company where you're applying. Where you live matters, too. The larger the city and the higher the cost of living, the more likely you'll receive a bigger salary.

Express your appreciation and strong interest in the job. Request at least 24 hours to consider it, even when saying "yes." Ask any questions you need clarified. Assess the job offer in terms of your needs, benefits and long-term career and life goals. Talk it over with someone you respect. Make a list of the pros and cons of the job offer.

"The job search these days drags on longer and longer. When you finally obtain that offer after weeks and weeks (and in some cases, months), it's not unusual to want to accept it right on the spot," writes Hansen on his website. "But even the best offers should be reviewed when you have a clear head — and without the pressure of your future boss or HR director staring at you. Most employers are willing to give you some time to contemplate a job offer — typically several days to a week."

Make sure the job description is clear. Note your reporting relationships, authority and advancement potential. Keep asking questions until you clearly understand. Careful thought and consideration will only gain you respect.

If you want the job, make it clear to the employer. If you're uncertain, state there are some items you'd like to discuss before you can accept the job and suggest meeting further to talk about the offer.

Focus your negotiations on a couple of items that are priorities for you. Items that could be negotiable include salary, benefits, tuition, training and vacation time, as well as a flexible schedule, stock options, company car, onsite day care and parking privileges. A compensation package is not just a salary. It includes health care and many other benefits that may be of greater value to you than a higher salary.

Today, many job seekers want good health insurance more than any other benefit. Ask what policies are available to you with the employer and then, on your own, consider how much that insurance would cost you with another employer with a weaker policy.

If you want more vacation time or a more flexible schedule, you may have to give up a little compensation — and you will have to decide if that's a deal you can live with.

Negotiations should never become emotional or hostile. Use your value, skills, experience and education to negotiate. Listen carefully. If the offer is less than you expected, let them know and state you're still interested in the position if they want to reconsider their offer. Don't assume the first offer is fixed even if the interviewer tells you it is.

If the same figure is offered a couple days later you can ask for a salary review in six months to evaluate your performance to determine if a salary bump is in order. Or, you can turn down the job while maintaining cheerful relations by asking that they keep you in mind for future openings paying a larger salary.

When you reach an agreement, request a document in writing and study it to make sure it contains the agreed upon points. And then have a celebration.

How to Succeed on the Job

Once you've made the big transition from job searching to landing the job, your next goal is job success. There are specific skills you need to know and use to be successful at your new position. Start by checking with your supervisor to

---

PROFILE:

TIPS FOR NEGOTIATING A HIGHER SALARY

When Tom Bjorgum finally found a job in the nation's worst recession in decades, he liked everything about it except one thing: the salary.

The company that eventually hired him, a power transmission distributor, offered a salary half the amount he once earned. Bjorgum, 59, figured he could negotiate a higher annual salary and a better deal on the bonus payout that occurred twice a year.

A few advantages played into his favor, among them a distinguished career in engineering sales and a potential employer who wanted someone to start quickly in the newly created job. It did not hurt, either, that two competitors for the position were dropped for different reasons.

And Bjorgum had a good argument.

"I did some research on salaries of sales engineers in the Twin Cities. It showed the average was $83,000 a year," he says. "That helped in negotiations. I figured I was in the driver's seat because I had interviewed with the president of the company, and I felt there was a sense of urgency to get someone in to start selling. It was good timing for me."

With the salary data in hand and his new employer needing to ignite some sales, Bjorgum asked for $10,000 to be added to his salary and for a larger percent in bonuses. The employer agreed to the terms. "I did the research online and I gave it to them," he says. "I thought the job was mine to lose, but I wasn't trying to be greedy."

determine your most important tasks and on what attributes you will be judged in reviews. Employers say more people lose their job due to poor work habits, rather than inability to do the work. The following suggestions are based on feedback culled from employers.

Employer Expectations

A positive attitude is one of the most important factors in achieving job success. Don't carry negative feelings into your new workplace. Deal with those emotions elsewhere.

Always be on time. How long will it take to get to work? Allow a few extra minutes for traffic problems and getting children to child care. Set an alarm clock to help you get up. Reliability and dependability will help you gain trust and respect from your new employer.

Strive for good attendance. If you need to be out sick, ask your supervisor the proper method of notification.

Know and follow all workplace rules, policies and procedures. Read the employee manuals.

Listen and learn. Be open to new ways of doing things, even if you were taught differently in school or on a different job. Don't be quick to find fault, criticize or complain until you can prove you can do something a better way.

Meet and exceed your employer's expectations. And if the expectations aren't clear, ask your employer to define them.

Learn all you can about your job before thinking about moving up the career ladder. Keep in mind you might not enjoy every aspect of your new job. Overcoming challenges at work may be still more appealing than not having a job at all. Now, let's look at several crucial areas in job performance.

Communication

A key component of any job is communication. When you need to talk with your supervisor, ask when would be a good time to meet. Consider your performance reviews opportunities for personal growth. Ask how you can improve. Most supervisors appreciate employees who are concerned about performance and want to improve. Your job success is also their success.

Ask for help when you need it. If you make a mistake, let your supervisor know immediately. Find out how you can fix it. Follow the proper chain of command. Discuss issues with your supervisor first.

Personal

Prior to starting the job, complete all of your appointments with doctors, dentists and others. Have an emergency plan for child care and transportation.

Be willing to learn new skills. Keep a record of classes you're taking that relate to the job. Review this with your supervisor when appropriate.

Take time in making new friends. Find positive and upbeat coworkers. Avoid negative, critical and gossiping people.

Be clean and well-groomed. Wear clean and job-appropriate clothes. Pay attention to how your coworkers are dressed. Avoid wearing strong perfumes or colognes.

Keep your personal life and problems at home. Don't use the employer's equipment and time for checking personal e-mail, making personal phone calls, using the copy machine or resolving your personal problems on the job. If you're having trouble resolving personal problems, counseling, support groups or employee assistance programs may be useful.

Be patient with yourself and your employer. It takes time to become familiar with a new job and learn the ins and outs. It often takes a good six months before you understand and feel comfortable with every task, your team members, clients and responsibilities.

If an opportunity presents itself you should volunteer for projects and committees if your supervisor approves. These experiences will give you a chance to exercise talents that aren't required in your current position and help you create a larger network of contacts within a company if your volunteer role is internal. In case of an external volunteer assignment, you will see the same advantages while building a professional network of contacts that could help you find a job in the future.

Getting Along With Others

Always respect diversity in the workplace, recognizing that people with different backgrounds often come together to produce better outcomes.

Accept criticism as constructive. Don't become defensive or take criticism personally. Thank people for their input. Consider changing your behavior if it's warranted. If you're unsure how to handle a situation, check with your supervisor. Always be friendly to everyone and be willing to go the extra mile. This creates goodwill with employers, coworkers and customers.

Notice who your boss respects and model yourself after them. Find a mentor, someone who knows the employer and the job well enough to coach you or show you the ropes.

Show appreciation. Let your supervisor(s) know you appreciate their training, support, input and feedback. Some bosses want to hear, too, real results that may not be favorable to them, or you. That requires a level of honesty that can be difficult to display but is intrinsic to your success and that of your employer.

Strive to be positively recognized.

Be a team player. Be willing to help. Know the goals of your job and how your job fits into the overall organization. Avoid a know-it-all attitude. Try to fit in with the team. Keep your sense of humor.

Final Thoughts

In today's world, a job search isn't usually a one-time event in most people's work life. Studies show that the average person will change jobs more frequently than in the past. People used to believe once they had secured a job with good pay and benefits, they would stay 20 to 30 years to retirement, but this is rarely true anymore.

The change is due, in part, to the fluctuating economy and fast-paced technological and scientific advances combined with international competition. That's why it's so important to learn job search techniques and to consider them an invaluable and evolving lifetime skill. Job search skills need to be constantly maintained and updated throughout your work life — even when you're employed. After you get a job you should maintain the following traits:

Keep your options open. See what your job skills are worth in the job market.

Get the training or experience you will need to move up or out.

Keep a list of awards, accomplishments and recognitions to present to your supervisor to lobby for a raise or promotion.

Layoffs and downsizings, after all, can come unexpectedly. That's why it's important to remain updated and networked in your profession even when times are good. While you do not want to have a job and then live in constant fear that it will be taken away, you may want to remain on alert by keeping your skill set and your network current because the future is unpredictable. As Yogi Berra once said: "It's tough to make predictions, especially about the future."

ENDNOTES: Thank You Notes

*T*he following are examples you can use as templates in different hiring situations.

THANK YOU LETTER SAMPLE

Your Name
(Address/phone/e-mail)

August 24, 2010

Mr. James Business
Human Resource Manager
ABC Company
111 Employment Way
Anytown, MN 55555

Dear Mr. Business:

Our conversation on August 24 gave me a better understanding of ABC Company and the requirements of the administrative assistant position. The additional information provided by Max and Katherine helped me gain a more complete perspective of the company's values and the job requirement. ABC clearly values positive and highly motivated employees, which are both qualities that I would bring to the job.

As my resume demonstrates, I have strong office and interpersonal skills, have proficiency with the software you use and enjoy the customer service experience you require. I am certain I can make a significant contribution to your company based on my past success as a detail- and results-oriented professional.

Meeting the office staff and touring the facility also reinforced my enthusiasm for this position. I would consider it a privilege to join your team and look forward to hearing your hiring decision. Thank you for the opportunity to discuss my potential for the administrative assistant position at your company. Please contact me if you have any additional questions.

Sincerely,

Amy Applicant

THANK YOU NOTE SAMPLES

February 28, 2010

Dear Ms. Smith,

It was a pleasure meeting you and Mr. Jones during our interview on Tuesday morning. Lourd's Industries sounds like the perfect place for me to apply my skills, especially since you use the WXY system, the same system I have been supporting the past three years. My proven track record and accomplishments with cost-effective systems can be an asset to your company.

Thank you for considering me for the accounting position. I will contact you by Tuesday of next week to learn of your decision. I look forward to the possibility of joining your staff.

Sincerely,

July 28, 2010

Dear Mr. Jones,

Based on our conversation this morning, my interest in working for Luke Industries is stronger than ever. The more I learn about Luke Industries, the more confident I am my skills can add to your company's success. Thank you for the opportunity to interview for the accounting position. I will contact you by Tuesday of next week to learn of your decision.

Sincerely,

RESPONSE TO REJECTION LETTER SAMPLE

Neda Job
Rural Route 1
Frostbite Falls, MN 55555
June 2, 2010

I. M. Boss
Human Resources Manager
Legitimate Business Services
123 Pinnacle Heights
Lake Wobegon, MN 55555

Dear Ms. Boss:

Thank you for the letter regarding your hiring decision for the
bookkeeping position. I was looking forward to joining your growing
company, and I am disappointed to hear your decision was not in my
favor at this time. I hope you will keep my qualifications in mind for any
future positions as bookkeeper or other related jobs.

Thank you again for your consideration, time and response. I hope
we will have the opportunity to connect again in the near future. Best
wishes on your upcoming sales.

Sincerely,

KEY JOB-HUNTING
WEBSITES AND SOURCES

 $\mathcal{T}$ he following websites and sources provide valuable information that you can use in your job search. They include job listings, Minnesota WorkForce Center locations, career and education information, and occupational data.

MINNESOTA CAREER SITES

MINNESOTAWORKS.NET
www.MinnesotaWorks.net

The most expansive job site in the state allows for searches by profession and ZIP code.

MINNESOTA WORKFORCE CENTERS
www.PositivelyMinnesota.com/wfc

The Minnesota Department of Employment and Economic Development sponsors about 50 WorkForce Centers where unemployed Minnesotans can receive job search assistance, including jobs data and classes on resume writing and interviewing. A list of the WorkForce Centers and career information are available at the agency's website.

ISEEK
www.iseek.org

Sponsored by Minnesota State Colleges and Universities, the site lists jobs and offers career and educational information.

CRAIGSLIST
www.craigslist.com

This famous grab bag of community information and sales includes job sections for the Twin Cities, Mankato, Fargo/Moorhead, Brainerd, Bemidji, Rochester, St. Cloud, Duluth and southwest Minnesota.

JOBS HQ
www.jobshq.com/

Jobs HQ has job listings for four states: Minnesota, South Dakota, North Dakota and Wisconsin.

LEAGUE OF MINNESOTA CITIES
www.lmc.org/page/1/careers.jsp

The League of Minnesota Cities has a good list of openings in municipalities around Minnesota.

MINNESOTA CAREER SITES (continued)

JEWISH VOCATIONAL SERVICES
www.jvsmn.org/index2.html
The non-denominational site has plenty of job information and a job search function.

JOB-HUNT.ORG
www.job-hunt.org/jobs/minnesota.shtml
This is a national site with a useful Minnesota subsection that links to many sites listed on this page.

MINNESOTAJOBS.COM
www.minnesotajobs.com
The site matches employers with employees in the state. It's free for job seekers and allows people to upload resumes.

MINNEAPOLIS STAR TRIBUNE
www.startribune.com
The state's largest newspaper and online news provider has an active jobs site.

ST. PAUL PIONEER PRESS
www.twincities.com
The Pioneer Press online site has plenty of ads for different professions.

NATIONAL CAREER SITES

CAREERONESTOP
www.careeronestop.org
Sponsored by the U.S. Department of Labor, the site offers tools to help job seekers, students, businesses and career professionals.

CAREER OVERVIEW
www.careerview.com
This site provides career and job information for dozens of professions.

O*NET
www.onetcenter.org/
O*NET offers occupational data.

GENERAL JOB SITES

CAREER BUILDER
www.careerbuilder.com

WALL STREET JOURNAL
CareerJournal.com

EMPLOYMENT 911
www.employment911.com

INDEED
www.indeed.com

JOB.COM
www.job.com

**JOBCENTRAL
NATIONAL LABOR EXCHANGE**
www.jobcentral.com

JOBDIG
www.jobdig.com

NATIONJOB
www.nationjob.com

MONSTER
www.monster.com

SIMPLY HIRED
www.SimplyHired.com

YAHOO! HOT JOBS
hotjobs.yahoo.com

Editor's Note: These and other websites cited in Creative Job Search are current as of press time. We recognize that new websites are continuously being created, and we encourage readers to pursue new sources of information as a part of their job search strategy.